TABLE OF CONTENTS

Unless otherwise indicated, all Scripture quotations are taken from the King James Version of the Bible.
The Holy Spirit Handbook · ISBN 1-56394-077-9/B-100
Copyright © 1990 by **MIKE MURDOCK**
All publishing rights belong exclusively to Wisdom International
Publisher/Editor: Deborah Murdock Johnson
Published by The Wisdom Center · 4051 Denton Hwy. · Ft. Worth, Texas 76117
USA · 1-817-759-BOOK · 1-817-759-0300
You Will Love Our Website...! www.WisdomOnline.com

Accuracy Department: To our Friends and Partners...We welcome any comments on errors or misprints you find in our book...Email our department: AccuracyDept@thewisdomcenter.tv. Your aid in helping us excel is highly valued.

The Holy Spirit Is
The Mystery
For Which Everyone
Is Searching.

-MIKE MURDOCK

WHY I WROTE THIS BOOK

————→﹥·O·﹤←————

My life changed dramatically on July 13, 1994.

It happened on a Wednesday morning. I had gone to bed at 5:00 a.m. after working all night long on a very special project. Two hours later, at 7:00 a.m., I was awakened suddenly and completely. An unexplainable, undeniable and awesome Presence was in my room.

Something more powerful than anything I had ever experienced...like an invisible emotional current was pulling me from my bedroom toward my "Secret Place." (This is my private prayer room in a small complex next to my house.) Now, I did not really call it "The Secret Place" at that time. It was simply my Prayer Room. But, that day was to change my understanding of God forever.

Because of the overwhelming and compelling urge to enter into intercession and go to The Secret Place, I thought that perhaps my father had suddenly passed on to be with the Lord. You see, my 91-year-old father is the greatest intercessor I have known in my lifetime. When I think of my dad, I think of him on his knees, with his hands raised, eyes closed and praying "in the Spirit." It was normal for him to spend six to ten hours a day in his personal and private prayer room. Throughout my entire life, I have never heard my father curse, lie or say a single word that could not be placed on the front of any newspaper in the world. That has always impressed me. He walks with God. Well, I had asked the Lord for many years to put his

Mantle of Prayer over my life.

When this incredible, unexplainable and compelling surging current began to *draw me toward The Secret Place,* I thought the Mantle was being transferred that morning. But, I couldn't feel any real sorrow had he really passed away. There was incredible calm and peace.

So, my second thought was, "Someone must be praying for me." You see, my entire ministry is held up daily by hundreds of people who call my name to God. I need their prayers, their intercession and their spiritual support more than any finances or even words of encouragement. I have built my entire ministry on Matthew 18:18-19, and the Prayer of Agreement. Somehow, from my childhood I received unshakable faith that when two people would pray for something *in the will of God,* every demon in hell had to submit to this penetrating power. God answers prayer. Quite simply.

When I travel, I often ask the audiences to remember "Mike Murdock in prayer every day. In fact, every time you walk into a grocery store and see a little bag of M & M's—let that be a reminder to call the name of Mike Murdock in prayer." Everyone always laughs aloud, but they get the point. And, many have told me over the years that every time they see a little bag of M & M candy, they immediately remember to call my name in prayer. So, I thought that somebody had just interceded and had a break-through in prayer for my life because of the over-whelming atmosphere and Presence in my room.

My third thought was more dramatic:
Could this be the burning bush experience I had wanted from the Lord my entire lifetime? I've always

admired ministers who experience visitations from angels. Wow! I have begged God in my early years to "please let me *see* an angel, *talk* to an angel." That seemed to be something so remarkable and life changing. I will never forget having supper with the late Roland Buck who had remarkable encounters with angels. But, these kinds of visitations never happened to me.

Yet, I have always believed that God can give you dramatic encounters that create an unshakable, unmovable confidence in His Assignment for your life—*something that no man can ever make you doubt.* He did it for the apostle Paul, when his name was Saul, on the Damascus road. He did it for Peter when He sent an angel in to the prison while the church prayed for him. He did it for Moses. The burning bush episode was never doubted, even when people were complaining around him many years later.

God is a *dramatic* God.

God is an *emotional* God.

God creates *unforgettable encounters*.

Normally, upon awakening, I would punch "play" on the tape recorder beside my bed or in my bathroom. I always listen to Scriptures being read while I dress. (Nothing on earth is as important as The Word of God being spoken into your mind, heart and life...every single day. *Nothing.*)

But, this surging, invisible and compelling current was overpowering me. Literally, I felt that time was of such essence—I didn't take time to even turn on the Scripture tape.

I grabbed my clothes. Pulling them on, I took my Bible and rushed out the door. I bounded down the concrete steps beside my swimming pool and crossed the driveway over to the little "guest house complex" next door. (I had turned it into private offices for myself, away from the ministry offices.)

It was the most dramatic day of my lifetime.

I fell in love with The Holy Spirit...as a Person. Not an experience. Not feeling His power surge through me. Rather, beholding His countenance, His glory, and finding Him to be the Best Friend I would ever have in my life.

Now, I am not merely a religious man with religious experiences. Neither am I a novice in the things of God.

My father and mother were married 63 years. She recently went to be with the Lord. My dad has been a pastor and minister for 62 years or so. I am the third child of a proven, established and precious man of God. Seven children are in our family today. My father is an intercessor. I was raised in a non-stop, continuous atmosphere of praise, worship and continuous prayer life. In my own mind, I remember seeing my father more on his knees than I ever saw him off his knees.

He always had a private room for prayer. Though some of us children had to pile up in one bedroom, Daddy always had his separate room for prayer. (It never occurred to me to question it. That was an accepted habit in our household. Daddy was always in his Prayer Room.)

Now, I also had a powerful and unforgettable encounter with The Holy Spirit at the age of ten. Many call it "the baptism of The Holy Spirit." It was at the altar in Franklin, Louisiana, that I was encouraged by a lady evangelist and her husband, Paul and Alice Cormier, to pursue "the baptism." This was basically considered to be an overwhelming encounter with The Holy Spirit that was accompanied by "an unknown prayer language."

I will never forget it. It was real, wonderful and genuine. Great joy entered my heart. And I was so thrilled that I could tell everyone at the church, at last, I had "experienced the baptism." Then, several years later, about the age of 15 or 16, I experienced another mighty and unforgettable baptism in The Holy Spirit in Beaumont, Texas. This happened on the platform when a wonderful man of God, Harry Hodge, prayed over my life on the platform at the church called Sabine Tabernacle.

But, *none of these experiences can compare with July 13, 1994.*

As I review my entire spiritual journey, I perceive that the body of Christ has an obsession with new spiritual experiences, encouragers and memorable events. There is nothing unholy or unspiritual about this. Most great champions of faith can trace the turning points of their life to a night with God, like Jacob had at Bethel.

Whether you experience unusual laughter, falling under the power of God called "slain in the Spirit" or simply running around a church building in response to the flow of joy...*every experience that brings you closer to God should be celebrated.* Every one of them.

Remember, too, that satan creates memorable experiences. He is an imitator of God, not a Creator. So, everything God does, satan tries to duplicate. I am thankful for every remarkable encounter that has swept me *towards* God's presence.

However, experiences are *never* enough.

Your experience should bring you *to Him.* If your

spiritual encounter does not bond you with The Holy Spirit, it has merely been an experience.

1. The Holy Spirit Is The One Who Changes You. Any experience with Him will create a noticeable difference in your conduct, behavior and even the words that flow from your mouth.

Sometimes, it seems that the church sees The Holy Spirit as the wonderful proprietor of a grocery store of blessings. Just like grocery stores sell candy, fruit and many wonderful "gifts," too many are coming away from His power and experiences discussing the "toys and candy."

The Holy Spirit does not want His gifts and manifestations to mesmerize you, paralyze you and become your focus.

2. He Expects You To Listen To Him Continuously.

3. He Expects You To Glorify Jesus In Your Life.

Most of us are like the inexperienced country kid visiting a city market for the first time. We are trance-like in our response and never stay around the store long enough to know the proprietor...who makes it all happen.

I would trade every discovery of my lifetime (including my knowledge of the alphabet) for what I discovered about The Holy Spirit on July 13, 1994.

My life changed in many ways.

My attitude changed forever.

The searching ended.

That invisible quest for "answers" stopped. I knew I had just found "The Answer" to every important question of life. The unrest stopped. The discontentment was over.

I lost all fear of man and what men could do to me. Every ounce of fear regarding any potential failure dissolved into nothing. I lost completely, the fear of criticism. The need for encouragement and affirmation from others evaporated. (It simply ceased to add anything to me for someone to compliment me in any way.) It didn't matter any more. His opinion alone mattered.

He was enough.

His presence, pleasing and pleasuring Him and the look on His countenance has become my *obsession.*

Two statements soon came from my lips that had never been uttered before in my whole lifetime. But, I was able to make after July 13, 1994:

First, when one of my best friends called and asked me how things were going, I had to honestly make this statement to him. Never, in 50 years of living, had I ever made such a statement. *"I don't know how Heaven could possibly be better than this earth."* That almost sounds blasphemous. How could anyone say such a thing with all the problems on earth? Simple—I could not feel any pain whatsoever, emotionally, mentally, financially or spiritually, of anything going on in my life. Things were in bad shape in some areas—but I could not *feel any of the pain or discomfort from it.* Today, I know why this happened. You see, everybody shouts and gets excited over Heaven. It is quite acceptable to believe that it's not streets of gold in Heaven that makes everyone happy. It is the presence of God. The Holy Spirit, Jesus, the Father—it is *their presence* that makes Heaven a Heaven.

Well, if this is really true—*then His presence on earth could keep us just as happy now*...before we ever leave here...if we are focused *totally* on Him.

Now, there have been days and some weeks since then that my focus has been *broken*. Earth contains warfare. Heaven does not. So, our inner battle here is to maintain total focus on Him *continuously*. In Heaven, no distractions exist.

Second, I was able to make a statement to him that was a first again—*"I cannot think of anything that could possibly improve my life."* Can you imagine such arrogance or pride or bliss? But it was true. This was incredibly unusual for me. I am in constant pursuit of excellence. There has never been a day in my life that I could not think of many things to improve my life! Hundreds! But, after developing an obsession with The Holy Spirit and His presence, it has occurred and been very true. *Nothing else on earth is really necessary for your total joy* (Psalm 16:11).

I looked into the face of a pastor friend some months ago. He asked, "What are your goals and dreams for your ministry? Where do you see your ministry going in the coming years? What is your vision and dream?"

I thought for a good while before answering him. I knew my answer might be misunderstood or misinterpreted. I wasn't trying to be cocky and arrogant. I knew that my answer would make me sound very prideful. But, I went ahead and told him my heart.

"I am already there. There is nothing else I'm obsessed in trying to do or achieve. I am *already* where I have been wanting to go."

He looked stunned.

"Are you telling me that you have *arrived?"* He looked incredulous and shocked. Actually, disbelieving.

Well, I knew that this did not show my humble side at all. But, I had to be honest with him.

"Yes," I replied slowly. "Yes, I suppose I *have* arrived."

"I've never heard anybody in my entire life say that they had arrived!"

"Well, don't get mad at everybody for it. Everyone ought to know if they have arrived at where they've been going!" I laughed.

Then I continued, "Let me explain. I wrote a song like this, 'You are where I have been going! Holy Spirit, You've been my destination all this time.'"

Everything inside you is moving toward something. The *success* teachers tell us it is a dream to be birthed. *Relationship* teachers tell us that it is a "soul mate." *Religious* leaders teach that you are in search of "the meaning of life." Philosophers focus on "your *destiny.*"

Your quest is for The Holy Spirit.

He created you. He formed you. He skillfully sculptured your life. You are *empty* unless He enters your life. You are *blind* unless He opens your eyes. You are *deaf* to the incredible sounds on earth unless He unlocks your ears. You are *lost* unless He reveals the way.

The Holy Spirit is the mystery for which everyone is searching. He is the Person Jesus told us to wait for, *look* for...that would continue His presence on the earth, after His ascension.

Now, some of the occurrences on that Wednesday morning, July 13, are "unlawful for me to utter." The Holy Spirit will not permit me to discuss them in detail. Perhaps it is my private "burning bush" encounter. Some of the details must be withheld.

Sometimes, The Holy Spirit gives us special secrets between us and Him—that's what makes the relationship so different and unique with Him.

However, there is not a single doubt in me that I have found the *Greatest Secret of the Universe*—the constant presence of The Holy Spirit will satisfy you beyond your imagination. He is who you are looking for. I know it *without a doubt*.

I call Him, "the One who stayed."

Now, I'm not a theologian. I understand little about the mystery of the Godhead. Those who claim great knowledge about the Godhead seem to be joyless. I refuse to be mentored by The Unhappy. I *do* believe...Jesus is making intercession in Heaven for us today and He assigned One who would never leave us nor forsake us, The Holy Spirit. This is only a small portion of my personal studies. It's not exhaustive, but I felt you'd want to get started...now.

That's why I wrote this book.

Mike Murdock

≈ 1 ≈
THE HOLY SPIRIT IS A PERSON

He Is Not Wind, Fire Or A White Dove.
Jesus knew this. He taught us, "And I will pray the Father, and He shall give you another Comforter, that He may abide with you for ever," (John 14:16).
He is not an "it."
He is..."Him."
You see, the pictures, metaphors and emblems used in the Bible can easily be misinterpreted and distorted.
He is a Person, not merely a presence. He is a Person who has a presence, an atmosphere emanating from Him. I think the word "Spirit" confuses many.
"Oh, she has such a wonderful *spirit* about her!" said a minister's wife to me. She was referring to the *attitude* of another lady.
"Oh, I love the *spirit* in this church!" This kind of statement refers to the atmosphere and climate existing in a building.
But, The Holy Spirit is not an attitude, atmosphere or environment. He is a Person who talks, thinks, plans and is incredibly brilliant and articulate. He is the *voice* of the Godhead to us. Read John 16:13, "He shall not speak of Himself; but whatsoever He shall hear, that shall He speak." A presence or an atmosphere does not talk! A *person* speaks.
A presence or an atmosphere does not have a

will, a mind, or a *plan*. Thoughts have presence. Animals generate a presence. But, *The Holy Spirit is much more than a presence.* You see, aroma is not really the food. The stink is not the skunk! The bark is not the dog. The quack is not the duck.

His presence is *evidence* of His Person.

Few people know this. That's why they never discuss their problems with Him. Most believe that He is a silent cloud or wind receiving assignments to different buildings or people.

Jesus recognized Him as a mentor. "He shall teach you all things," (John 14:26).

He is not merely a fog.

He is not merely a wind.

He is not merely fire.

He is not merely rain.

He is not merely a white dove at a baptismal service. If He were wind, He could not mentor men. If He were a white bird, He could not teach you all the sayings of Jesus (John 14:26). If He were merely fire, He could not impart counsel. The Holy Spirit simply uses various pictures of Himself to reveal His workings, His nature and various qualities about Himself.

The Holy Spirit can enter your life like water— refreshing you. "For I will pour water upon him that is thirsty, and floods upon the dry ground: I will pour My Spirit upon thy seed, and My blessing upon thine offspring: And they shall spring up as among the grass, as willows by the water courses," (Isaiah 44:3-4).

The Holy Spirit can enter your life like fire— purifying you. "And there appeared unto them cloven tongues like as of fire, and it sat upon each of them. And they were all filled with the Holy Ghost, and began to speak with other tongues, as the Spirit gave them utterance," (Acts 2:3-4).

The Holy Spirit can move suddenly and quickly in your life—like wind.   "And suddenly there came a sound from heaven as of a rushing mighty wind, and it filled all the house where they were sitting," (Acts 2:2).

The Holy Spirit will come to you the way that you need Him the most.   He can come as a gentle *Nurturer*—like a mother nurturing her starving and dependent child.   He can come as a brilliant and articulate *Advisor*—when you are facing a difficult decision.   He can come as a comforting *Healer*—when you have been scarred and tormented from a battle.

The Holy Spirit is a Person.   When you embrace this, your Christian experience will change dramatically, instantly and satisfy every part of your heart and life.

Always remember, The Holy Spirit is a Person.

Our Prayer Together...

"Father, teach me to walk and live with my Mentor, my Companion, The Holy Spirit. You are not fire, wind or rain. You are the Holy One who created me. In Jesus' name. Amen."

Your Change Of Behavior Is
Not The Price Of
Your Relationship With Him,
But The Product Of
Your Intimacy With Him.

-MIKE MURDOCK

2

THE HOLY SPIRIT IS THE GIVER OF LIFE

Life Is A Priceless, Precious Gift To Us.

The Giver is The Holy Spirit. "But the Spirit giveth life," (2 Corinthians 3:6). "The Spirit gives life," (John 6:63 NIV).

The Holy Spirit impregnated Mary, the mother of Jesus. "Now the birth of Jesus Christ was on this wise: When as His mother Mary was espoused to Joseph, before they came together, she was found with child of the Holy Ghost. But while he thought on these things, behold, the angel of the Lord appeared unto him in a dream, saying, Joseph, thou son of David, fear not to take unto thee Mary thy wife: for that which is conceived in her is of the Holy Ghost," (Matthew 1:18, 20).

Think about this incredible truth. The Holy Spirit is the One who ushered in the entry of Jesus, the Son of God, into the earth.

Any words spoken by The Holy Spirit will bring life and energy into you. "The Spirit gives life; the flesh counts for nothing. The words I have spoken to you are spirit and they are life," (John 6:63 NIV).

The Holy Spirit is the life of God dwelling within you. "Even the Spirit of truth; whom the world cannot receive, because it seeth Him not, neither knoweth

Him: but ye know Him; for He dwelleth with you, and shall be in you," (John 14:17).

The Spirit of Life is one of the titles of The Holy Spirit. "For the law of the Spirit of life in Christ Jesus hath made me free from the law of sin and death," (Romans 8:2).

The Holy Spirit will breathe life into every person who died in Christ, at the coming of Christ. "But if the Spirit of Him that raised up Jesus from the dead dwell in you, He that raised up Christ from the dead shall also quicken your mortal bodies by His Spirit that dwelleth in you," (Romans 8:11).

The Holy Spirit considers you His dwelling place. "Know ye not that ye are the temple of God, and that the Spirit of God dwelleth in you?" (1 Corinthians 3:16).

The Holy Spirit is the Enabler that helps you to keep and protect any good thing God has given you. "That good thing which was committed unto thee keep by the Holy Ghost which dwelleth in us," (2 Timothy 1:14).

The Holy Spirit provides tenacity, strength and determination for those who become dependent on His Times of Refreshing acts and are addicted to His presence. Oh, He is the Source of life itself!

While I was dictating these very words, something glorious and precious happened. One of my associates walked into the Wisdom Room here at my home, as I was dictating this chapter, with good news: one of my mother sheep had just given birth to a beautiful little black sheep...with a white star on its forehead. I had to stop my dictation, rush out to the yard where all the animals were gathered around the little baby sheep. It was precious. Surrounding the mother and the little baby were many other animals that I have here at my home—several llamas were crowding in trying to nose the little one. Eleazar, my huge camel, wanted to have a part. Smoky, my little donkey, was trying to get his nose in the huddle as well. My antelope were watching from a distance...but it seemed that the entire yard of animals was feeling the glory of life itself—*life! You feel it in the air!*

I thought this was wonderful. While I was writing you about the Giver of all life, right here a few feet from me outside, something He created...a *first*... was just born.

Think for a moment. Look around you at the incredible animals—antelope, llamas, sheep, goats, camels and behold the incredible imagination of The Holy Spirit and the many ways *He sees methods to generate life and create life!*

I look into the trees, and I see beautiful white and blue-green peacocks here at my home. *The Holy Spirit thought of these.*

He created them.

As I look into my aquarium, I see beautiful multi-colored fish swimming smoothly through the water. They were created for the water. He thought of this.

The Holy Spirit is the Giver of all life.

The trees are beautiful today. New plants are springing forth. Flowers are beginning to bloom. The Holy Spirit has thought of a million ways to bring life into this earth.

You were His idea.

You are not alone.

You have a destiny.

You are on His mind all the time.

You are the focus of everything The Holy Spirit will do today.

Always remember, The Holy Spirit is the Giver of life.

Our Prayer Together...

"Precious Holy Spirit, thank You from the depths of my heart for bringing me into Your world. I *want* to be here. I *love* being here. I love *tasting* what You have created. I love *beholding*, *observing* and *gazing* upon the beauty that You have imagined and brought into being. Thank You for the beautiful animals, the trees, the birds around me. Thank You for my new little black sheep born just seconds ago. Thank You from the depths of my heart for letting me enjoy Your world.

"Show me *how to pleasure You in return*. You made me for greatness. You made me to bring pleasure to You. Draw me toward You, Holy Spirit. Draw me toward You today. In Jesus' name. Amen."

≈ 3 ≈
THE HOLY SPIRIT CREATED YOU

You Are His Greatest Product.

Job knew this. "The Spirit of God hath made me, and the breath of the Almighty hath given me life," (Job 33:4).

Your personality, body and everything about you is the design of The Holy Spirit. Think of this incredible body that functions miraculously. "I will praise Thee; for I am fearfully and wonderfully made: marvellous are Thy works; and that my soul knoweth right well," (Psalm 139:14).

Your body is the temple of The Holy Spirit. "What? know ye not that your body is the temple of the Holy Ghost which is in you, which ye have of God, and ye are not your own?" (1 Corinthians 6:19).

The Holy Spirit was involved in the creative designing of the temple through Solomon. "And the pattern of all that he had by the Spirit, of the courts of the house of the Lord, and of all the chambers round about, of the treasuries of the house of God, and of the treasuries of the dedicated things," (1 Chronicles 28:12).

The Holy Spirit was involved in the creation of the earth at the beginning. "And the earth was without form, and void; and darkness was upon the face of the deep. And the Spirit of God moved upon the face of the waters," (Genesis 1:2).

The Holy Spirit is the One sent to form new creations on earth. "Thou sendest forth Thy Spirit, they are created: and Thou renewest the face of the earth," (Psalm 104:30).

The Holy Spirit appears to be the One who decides the very shape of every animal. "By His Spirit He hath garnished the heavens; His hand hath formed the crooked serpent," (Job 26:13).

The Holy Spirit is the spirit of life within you that keeps you living and breathing every single moment. "The Spirit of God hath made me, and the breath of the Almighty hath given me life," (Job 33:4). "Thus saith the Lord God unto these bones; Behold, I will cause breath to enter into you, and ye shall live: And I will lay sinews upon you, and will bring up flesh upon you, and cover you with skin, and put breath in you, and ye shall live; and ye shall know that I am the Lord. And shall put My Spirit in you, and ye shall live, and I shall place you in your own land: then shall ye know that I the Lord have spoken it, and performed it, saith the Lord," (Ezekiel 37:5-6, 14).

The Holy Spirit also is the One who gives you the new life after your second birth, the regeneration. "Not by works of righteousness which we have done, but according to His mercy He saved us, by the washing of regeneration, and renewing of the Holy Ghost," (Titus 3:5).

The Holy Spirit is the Source of your life...every part of your life.

Always remember, The Holy Spirit created you.

∼ 4 ∼
THE HOLY SPIRIT IS THE AUTHOR OF THE WORD OF GOD

Your Bible Is His Gift To You.

The Holy Spirit breathed through men, the holy Scriptures. "For the prophecy came not in old time by the will of man: but holy men of God spake as they were moved by the Holy Ghost," (2 Peter 1:21).

When you quote the Bible, you are quoting The Holy Spirit. He is articulate, brilliant and authored the words of God to us today (2 Peter 1:21).

The Holy Spirit inspired holy men of God to write the Bible to correct those in error. "All scripture is given by inspiration of God, and is profitable for doctrine, for reproof, for correction, for instruction in righteousness: That the man of God may be perfect, throughly furnished unto all good works," (2 Timothy 3:16-17).

Oh, think of this glorious and incredible Bible we carry around every day! The Holy Spirit spoke every word through 40 people sensitive to Him, over a 1600 year period of time.

He wanted to breathe His *life* into you.

He wanted His *energy* to be poured through you.

He wanted His *Wisdom* deposited in your heart.

He wanted His *instincts* and nature to be evident and obvious in you.

He wanted you to *know what He knows*.

He wanted you to *feel what He feels*.

He wanted you to *see* what He is looking at.

The Holy Spirit gave you The Word of God as your special weapon, the sword of the Spirit. "And take the helmet of salvation, and the sword of the Spirit, which is the word of God," (Ephesians 6:17). It is the weapon of The Holy Spirit—the weapon He uses against satan. His *words* are His destructive weapons that destroy the things of satan.

Jesus used the weapon of The Word, the sword of the Spirit. When satan tempted Him, Jesus simply answered with the words of The Holy Spirit! "And Jesus answered him, saying, It is written, That man shall not live by bread alone, but by every word of God," (Luke 4:4).

The Holy Spirit led Jesus into the place where He would be tempted. Then, gave Him the weaponry (The Word of God) to use against satan. Satan was defeated and angels came to minister to Christ.

So, satan reacts instantly to any words of The Holy Spirit that you believe, embrace and stand on in total faith (Luke 4).

So, The Holy Spirit always anticipates your warfare. He understands battle. It matters to Him. Your winning is on His mind all the time. He truly has not left you comfortless. He has put His weapon in your *hand*, in your *mouth*, in your *life*.

Treasure His words today. The Word of God is the weapon satan cannot withstand.

Your Bible contains 66 books. These 66 books contain 1189 chapters. Someone estimated that you could read the entire Bible through within 56 hours. I encourage you to develop your relationship with The Holy Spirit by daily reading The Word of God.

5 Helpful Hints On Reading Your Bible

1. Establish A Daily Habit. When you read three chapters a day (and five on Sunday), you'll read the entire Bible through within twelve months. When you read nine chapters each day in the New Testament, you will finish the New Testament every 30 days. When you read 40 chapters a day, you will read the entire Bible every 30 days of your life!

2. Read At The Same Place Every Day. That should be your Secret Place, where you talk to The Holy Spirit. But, it should be a private and confidential place away from the traffic of everyone else. Places matter. *Where you are determines what grows in you.*

3. Read It At The Same Time Each Day. Habit is so powerful. Habits are more powerful than desires. Habit is a gift from God. It simply means that anything you do twice becomes easier. Stop thinking of the word "habit" as a bad word. It is a great word! It is God's easiest way to help you succeed.

4. Become A Passionate Expert On One Topic In The Bible. Focus and become knowledgeable about that center of your expertise. For example, if you want to study faith, circle every Scripture relating to faith in your personal Bible. Then, create a personal 365-Scripture calendar on the subject of faith. (If you decide to focus on becoming an expert in Scripture on The Holy Spirit—find 365 Scriptures that help you understand The Holy Spirit. Make that your legacy for your family, and teach them a Scripture a day in memorization time.)

5. Talk Scriptures In Every Conversation. You may be on the phone or in a business transaction—use the words of The Holy Spirit to answer someone. The Bible becomes your data base for your personal opinion.

The Word of God is the tool in the hand of The Holy Spirit to nurture you and furnish you everything you need to succeed on earth. "All scripture is given by inspiration of God, and is profitable for doctrine, for reproof, for correction, for instruction in righteousness: That the man of God may be perfect, throughly furnished unto all good works," (2 Timothy 3:16-17).

As you develop a consciousness of the *opinion* of The Holy Spirit (the Bible), your whole world will change.

Always remember, The Holy Spirit is the Author of The Word of God.

☙ 5 ❧

THE HOLY SPIRIT ALONE CAN IMPART THE UNSHAKABLE CONFIDENCE THAT CHRIST DWELLS WITHIN YOU

The Invisible Persuader Concerning Christ Is Within You.

Nobody else can persuade your mind so that you feel inner satisfaction. Articulate theologians cannot satisfy you. A pleading pastor cannot drive the doubts away.

It is The Holy Spirit Who confirms that Christ dwells within your heart and removes every doubt about Him. "Hereby know we that we dwell in Him, and He in us, because He hath given us of His Spirit," (1 John 4:13).

The apostle Paul, who encountered incredible warfare in his ministry and life, knew this. "The Spirit itself beareth witness with our spirit, that we are the children of God," (Romans 8:16).

Doubts are deadly. Nothing is more poisonous than the erratic and roller coaster emotions regarding your salvation. Satan will taunt, accuse and blame you for everything. He is the accuser of the brethren (Revelation 12:10). You must fall in love with The Holy Spirit to keep living this incredible life of peace and inner calm.

"I don't really know if I am saved or not," cried one teenager after church one night.

Her pastor pleaded with her to "just believe." Her parents felt baffled. Her Sunday school teacher tried walking her "through the Scriptures."

Nobody could persuade her that Christ was alive and well within her...*but The Holy Spirit could.*

As we began to pray together, I asked The Holy Spirit to *confirm* in her heart that she was truly a child of the Most High God, that Jesus had accepted her and lived within her. Within moments, her face changed. Her joy changed. A calm flowed across her countenance. She was born again...and she knew it *without a doubt.*

Her unshakable *confidence* about the in-dwelling Christ *came from The Holy Spirit.*

You may be encountering real temptations in your personal life. Your mind may experience torment over your failures and mistakes. Your conscience is hurting. Has Christ left you? Is your name really written as one of those who serve Him?

Nobody on earth can help you with this...but the wonderful and precious Adviser, The Holy Spirit. "And it is the Spirit that beareth witness, because the Spirit is truth. For there are three that bear record in heaven, the Father, the Word, and the Holy Ghost: and these three are one," (1 John 5:6-7).

Always remember, The Holy Spirit alone can impart the unshakable confidence that Christ dwells within you.

Our Prayer Together...

"Precious Holy Spirit, I pray for my dear friend this very moment who is encountering great inner turmoil. Confusion has entered. Your peace is not felt. I release You to work in this precious heart and life. Stop the storm. Bring the calm. Let Your peace that passeth all understanding dwell in this heart today. Confirm that my friend is truly born again...*without a shadow of doubt*. In Jesus' name. Amen."

Your Assignment Is
Not Your Decision,
But Your Discovery.

-MIKE MURDOCK

≫ 6 ≫

THE HOLY SPIRIT CHOOSES WHICH GIFTS, TALENTS AND SKILLS YOU RECEIVE FROM THE FATHER

The Holy Spirit Planted Greatness Within You.

The Holy Spirit is a gift. And the Giver of gifts. "If ye then, being evil, know how to give good gifts unto your children: how much more shall your heavenly Father give the Holy Spirit to them that ask Him?" (Luke 11:13).

The Holy Spirit put the gifts and talents within you. Natural and spiritual gifts! "Now there are diversities of gifts, but the same Spirit. And there are differences of administrations, but the same Lord. For to one is given by the Spirit the word of Wisdom; to another the word of knowledge by the same Spirit; To another faith by the same Spirit; to another the gifts of healing by the same Spirit," (1 Corinthians 12:4-5, 8-9).

The Holy Spirit decides if you get one, two or five talents. "But all these worketh that one and the selfsame Spirit, dividing to every man severally as He will," (1 Corinthians 12:11).

Every man receives different amounts of gifts and skills from The Holy Spirit. "And unto one He gave five talents, to another two, and to another one; to every man according to his several ability; and straightway took his journey," (Matthew 25:15).

You were planned by The Holy Spirit before your parents ever saw your face. "Before I formed thee in the belly I knew thee; and before thou camest forth out of the womb I sanctified thee, and I ordained thee a prophet unto the nations," (Jeremiah 1:5).

Destiny is to be discovered, not decided. God has already developed a plan for your life. You must enter His presence to discover it. "I know the thoughts that I think toward you," (Jeremiah 29:11).

Your gift may be music, writing, drawing or administration. Give attention to it. The Holy Spirit expects you to develop and grow your gift.

9 Important Facts Concerning Your Gifts, Talents And Skills

1. Remember Nobody Else Is Aware Of All The Gifts The Holy Spirit Has Placed Within You.

The teacher of famous opera singer, Enrico Caruso, said Caruso had no voice and could not sing.

Walt Disney was fired by a newspaper for "lacking ideas."

An expert said of famous football coach, Vince Lombardi: "He possesses minimal knowledge. Lacks motivation."

Regarding Fred Astaire—a 1933 memo from the MGM testing director said, "Can't act. Slightly bald. Can dance a little."

Louisa May Alcott, the author of the famous

book, *Little Women,* was told by her family that she should find a job as a servant or a seamstress.

The teacher of the famous musician, Beethoven, called him hopeless as a composer.

2.   Realize That Your Gifts May Not Surface Immediately But Over A Period Of Time. Eighteen publishers turned down Richard Bach's ten thousand word story about a soaring seagull before MacMillan finally published it in 1970. By 1975, *Jonathan Livingston Seagull* had sold more than seven million copies in the U.S. alone.

3.   Be Patient When Your Gifts Take Time And Seasons Of Preparation To Become Strong. Beethoven handled the violin awkwardly and preferred playing his own compositions instead of improving his technique.   "Study to shew thyself approved unto God," (2 Timothy 2:15).

4.   Do Not Be Discouraged If You Experience A Number Of Failures Before You Reach Your Place Of Destiny. Walt Disney went bankrupt several times before he built Disneyland. Most of your great achievers have collected a number of outstanding failures as well.

Look at the apostle Peter. He was weak, and intimidated by a woman at the home of the high priest. Yet, he became the great preacher on the day of Pentecost. Historians teach that when he died, he was crucified but asked that he be crucified upside down. He felt unworthy to be crucified like Jesus. "And let us not be weary in well doing: for in due season we shall reap, if we faint not," (Galatians 6:9). "For a just man falleth seven times and riseth up again," (Proverbs 24:16).

5. Use Your Gifts To Bless Those Closest To You Today. Some spend all their life looking around the earth for a place to "land." There is an old saying that few of us have really grasped: "Bloom where you're presently planted." "Withhold not good from them to whom it is due, when it is in the power of thine hand to do it," (Proverbs 3:27).

When you excel in your present situation, somebody "in the palace" will call for you as Pharaoh called for Joseph (Genesis 41:14).

6. Expect Your Gifts And Skills To Bring You Before Great Men. "Seest thou a man diligent in his business? he shall stand before kings; he shall not stand before mean men," (Proverbs 22:29). When Joseph interpreted the dream of the butler, it brought him before Pharoah. David came before Saul as a musician and song-writer.

7. Accept The Reality That Your Gifts May Not Be Celebrated By Those In Your Own Home. Joseph experienced this. His brothers did not recognize the gift of God within him. But, he knew that his ability to interpret dreams came from God. Jesus was misunderstood by His own family who did not believe (John 7:5), and even thought He was beside Himself (Mark 3:21). Never lose hope because "thy faith may become effectual by the acknowledging of every good thing which is in you," (Philemon 6).

8. Remind Others Of The Gifts Within You, Placed There By The Holy Spirit. It is not wrong to advertise. It is not wrong to tell others that your gifts are resident within you. When the butler left the prison where Joseph was the chief jailer, Joseph told him that he had done nothing to be there. And, he asked him to spread the word about him. The butler remembered two years later.

Jesus Himself promoted the gifts He possessed that could bless others. He told the woman at the well that He would give her water—she would never thirst again (John 4:14). "Know them which labour among you, and are over you," (1 Thessalonians 5:12).

9.   Invest In Seminars, Tapes Or Books Or Whatever It Takes To Develop Your Gifts And Skills. Seasons of preparation are in every achiever's life. Jesus took thirty years. Moses took eighty years. "Study to shew thyself approved," (2 Timothy 2:15).

Always remember, The Holy Spirit chooses which gifts, talents and skills you receive from the Father.

Our Prayer Together...

"Precious Holy Spirit, thank You for the wonderful gifts You have placed within us. Those gifts are *discerned* by us...by the things we love, hate, and grieve us. Thank You for the appetites and passions You planted deep within us. Reveal where our gifts are *most needed* today. *Open* doors. Enable us to recognize the Golden Connections around us and to quickly be obedient to *walk through those doors.* In Jesus' name. Amen."

God Had A Son
   But Wanted A Family;
He Sowed His Son
   To Create His Family.

-MIKE MURDOCK

7

THE HOLY SPIRIT IMPARTS INNER CONFIDENCE THAT YOU BELONG TO THE FAMILY OF GOD

Nobody Wants To Be On The Outside.

Something within you needs a sense of belonging. Everything God created requires a *connection*. Nothing He makes is whole. Everything is a *part*.

Your *eyes* need a view.

Your *ears* need sounds.

Your *mind* needs thoughts.

Your *mouth* needs words.

Your *feet* require a place to go.

Your *hands* will reach for something.

Something in you finds "*belonging*" necessary *for comfort*, satisfaction and rest.

The Holy Spirit is the only One who can give you the inner assurance that you truly are a child of God, belonging to this gigantic family of God. "For ye have not received the spirit of bondage again to fear; but ye have received the Spirit of adoption, whereby we cry, Abba, Father. The Spirit itself beareth witness with our spirit, that we are the children of God," (Romans 8:15-16). (By the way, Billy Graham wrote a great book on The Holy Spirit. In it, He explains the mistranslations that occurred here in the King James version of the word, "itself." In the original, the correct word is "Himself.")

You are not alone in this huge world today. Your focusing on discouraging things in your life may bring an inner sorrow and depression. But, *you are not forgotten by God.* He has kept you, preserved you and has great plans for you today.

Perhaps, you were not born into a wealthy family. Poverty may have stalked you during your entire life. You may remember the shame you felt when others could eat in nice restaurants, but you could not. Your father may be illiterate. Your own education may be limited. You may even feel ashamed to speak in front of other people. But, The Holy Spirit created you to be very special.

He *knows* where you belong.

He has uncommon plans for you.

He sowed the *Seeds of Greatness* in you while you were yet in your mother's womb.

So, when satan reminds you of past failures, remind him of his *future* failure. I like the tee-shirt I saw on a young man in the mall one day—"When satan reminds you of your past; remind him of his future."

Because you belong to the family of God, many benefits are awaiting you as you reach for them in faith. "And if children, then heirs; heirs of God, and joint-heirs with Christ; if so be that we suffer with Him, that we may be also glorified together," (Romans 8:17).

Get excited about the rewards of being in the family of God. *Favor* is going to flow toward your house today. *Healing and health* will be the watchword for this year. Sickness and disease can be defeated because you are His child appropriating the faith He has placed within you.

Stop the victim vocabulary. Let your words become photographs of the future you desire, instead of the future you fear.

Talk like an overcomer.

Think like an overcomer.

Laugh like a victor, not a victim.

Your heavenly Father has heard the cry of your heart. His biggest plans are coming to pass in your life.

Jesus wants you to pray as a child of God. When He taught the disciples to pray, He taught: "Our Father which art in heaven..." (Luke 11:2). He wants you to approach your Father as if you truly belong to Him—*because you do!*

God wants to be your Father even more than you want to be His child. "And will be a Father unto you, and ye shall be My sons and daughters, saith the Lord Almighty," (2 Corinthians 6:18).

God will pursue you, His people and His family. "I will call them My people, which were not My people; and her beloved, which was not beloved. And it shall come to pass, that in the place where it was said unto them, Ye are not My people; there shall they be called the children of the living God," (Romans 9:25-26).

The love of God for you, not religious conduct and behavior, makes the relationship possible. "Behold, what manner of love the Father hath bestowed upon us, that we should be called the sons of God: therefore the world knoweth us not, because it knew Him not. Beloved, now are we the sons of God, and it doth not yet appear what we shall be: but we know that, when He shall appear, we shall be like Him; for we shall see

Him as He is," (1 John 3:1-2). Your change of behavior is not the *price* of your relationship with Him, but the *product* of your intimacy with Him.

Belonging to God births a hope, and that hope will motivate you toward purification. "And every man that hath this hope in Him purifieth himself, even as He is pure" (1 John 3:3).

The Holy Spirit is sent into those who accept God as the Father. "And because ye are sons, God hath sent forth the Spirit of His Son into your hearts, crying Abba, Father. Wherefore thou art no more a servant, but a son; and if a son, then an heir of God through Christ," (Galatians 4:6-7).

Belonging to God will require your faith in Christ Jesus. "For ye are all the children of God by faith in Christ Jesus," (Galatians 3:26).

Your faith will grow as you speak and hear the Word of God continually. "Faith cometh by hearing, and hearing by the word of God," (Romans 10:17).

Always remember, The Holy Spirit imparts inner confidence that you belong to the family of God.

Our Prayer Together...

"Father, thank You for The Holy Spirit who has confirmed within our hearts that You are our Father, I am Your child, and I truly belong to the great family of God. In Jesus' name. Amen."

8

THE HOLY SPIRIT LOVES CONVERSATION

The Holy Spirit Is A Communicator.
When The Holy Spirit comes, your speech may change immediately. "And it shall come to pass afterward, that I will pour out My Spirit upon all flesh; and your sons and your daughters shall prophecy," (Joel 2:28; see also Acts 2:16-18).

The Holy Spirit affected the words of thousands on the Day of Pentecost. "And there appeared unto them cloven tongues like as of fire, and it sat upon each of them. And they were all filled with the Holy Ghost, and began to speak with other tongues, as the Spirit gave them utterance," (Acts 2:3-4).

The Holy Spirit was involved when Jesus gave commandments to the apostles before His ascension. "Until the day in which He was taken up, after that He through the Holy Ghost had given commandments unto the apostles whom He had chosen," (Acts 1:2).

The Holy Spirit influences your conversations with others. "But ye shall receive power, after that the Holy Ghost is come upon you: and ye shall be witnesses unto Me both in Jerusalem, and in all Judæa, and in Samaria, and unto the uttermost part of the earth," (Acts 1:8).

The Holy Spirit affects the boldness and aggressiveness of your conversations with others. "And when they had prayed, the place was shaken where they were assembled together; and they were all filled with the Holy Ghost, and they spake the word of God with boldness," (Acts 4:31).

The first proof and evidence of The Holy Spirit in your life is the change in your conversation. The Holy Spirit births a militant position on Jesus Christ. It was obvious in the life of Peter. He was weak and intimidated by others before Pentecost. Afterwards, he was bold and specific: "Then Peter, filled with the Holy Ghost, said unto them...Be it known unto you all, and to all the people of Israel, that by the name of Jesus Christ of Nazareth, whom ye crucified, whom God raised from the dead, even by Him doth this man stand here before you whole...Neither is there salvation in any other: for there is none other name under heaven given among men, whereby we must be saved. Now when they saw the boldness of Peter and John, and perceived that they were unlearned and ignorant men, they marvelled; and they took knowledge of them, that they had been with Jesus," (Acts 4:8-13).

The Holy Spirit talks more than any other person on earth. He knows *everybody.* He knows the personal weaknesses of every human He created. He can speak *every language.* He can *talk everywhere at the same time.* He can *speak to thousands simultaneously.* "He that hath an ear, let him hear what the Spirit saith unto the churches," (Revelation 2:7, 11, 17 and Revelation 3:6, 13, 22).

The Holy Spirit expects you to continuously listen for His voice. "To day if ye will hear His voice, Harden not your heart," (Psalm 95:7-8).

The Holy Spirit will teach you. "He shall teach you all things," (John 14:26).

The Holy Spirit will remind you of the principles of Jesus. "And bring all things to your remembrance, whatsoever I have said unto you," (John 14:26).

The Holy Spirit will convict you of sin in your life. "And when He is come, He will reprove the world of sin, and of righteousness, and of judgment," (John 16:8).

The Holy Spirit will talk to you about things in your future. "He will shew you things to come," (John 16:13).

The Holy Spirit will talk to you about those to whom you are assigned. "Then the Spirit said unto Philip, Go near, and join thyself to this chariot," (Acts 8:29).

The Holy Spirit will talk to you about the motives of others around you. "And the Spirit bade me go with them, nothing doubting," (Acts 11:12).

The Holy Spirit will talk to you about your specific Assignment. "As they ministered to the Lord, and fasted, the Holy Ghost said, Separate Me Barnabas and Saul for the work whereunto I have called them," (Acts 13:2).

The Holy Spirit will discuss the location and geographical area of your Assignment. "So they, being sent forth by the Holy Ghost, departed unto Seleucia; and from thence they sailed to Cyprus," (Acts 13:4).

The Holy Spirit knows where your gifts are most desperately needed (Acts 8).

The Holy Spirit knows the very person who can answer the questions that perplex you (Acts 8).

The Holy Spirit will link you miraculously with

those who will celebrate you (Acts 8).

The Holy Spirit will reveal those on whom judgment is falling. "Then Saul, (who also was called Paul,) filled with the Holy Ghost, set his eyes on him and said, O full of all subtilty and all mischief, thou child of the devil, thou enemy of all righteousness, wilt thou not cease to pervert the right ways of the Lord," (Acts 13:9-10).

The Holy Spirit reveals those who despise you as an enemy (Acts 13:9-10).

The Holy Spirit will reveal those who are filled with demon spirits (Acts 13:9-10).

The Holy Spirit will reveal to you the difference between the essential and nonessential issues. "For it seemed good to the Holy Ghost, and to us, to lay upon you no greater burden than these necessary things," (Acts 15:28).

The Holy Spirit will talk to you about the place of provision and supply. "Get thee hence, and turn thee eastward, and hide thyself by the brook...I have commanded the ravens to feed thee there," (1 Kings 17:3-4). This is evident here in the life of Elijah.

The Holy Spirit will talk to you about problems in the lives of other people. Samuel experienced this as a lad. God talked to him about Eli, his spiritual mentor.

The Holy Spirit within you will become a Source of agitation to unholy men (Acts 6:10).

That's why it's important for you to have a special place to meet with Him every day. I call my private place of prayer, The Secret Place.

You must move away from the voices of others when you really want to hear the voice of The Holy Spirit.

Solitude is necessary for *intimacy*.

Intimacy is necessary for *impartation*.

Impartation is necessary for *change*.

You can only change when The Holy Spirit is talking into your life.

4 Ways The Holy Spirit Will Speak To You

1.   The Holy Spirit Speaks To You Through Men And Women Of God. These wonderful people of God inspire our faith and correct your focus. When you obey the instructions of The Holy Spirit through a man of God, you will prosper beyond your imagination. "Believe in the Lord your God, so shall ye be established; believe His prophets, so shall ye prosper," (2 Chronicles 20:20). *The words of The Holy Spirit energize and bring life.* "It is the Spirit that quickeneth; the flesh profiteth nothing: the words that I speak unto you, they are spirit, and they are life," (John 6:63). Thank God for your pastor, the gift from The Holy Spirit to your life. He warns you. Comforts you.   Strengthens you.   Develop the discipline of church attendance—even when the busyness of your life overwhelms you. When you are exposed to the preaching of a man of God, the chances of your success are multiplied over and over.

2.   The Holy Spirit Speaks Through Your Conscience. When Stephen, full of faith and power, did great wonders and miracles among the people, some disputed with him. Their conscience reacted. "And they were not able to resist the wisdom and the spirit by which he spake," (Acts 6:10). They became so angry, they rose up and stoned this great man of God. The Holy Spirit used their own conscience to convict them.

3. The Holy Spirit Speaks To You Through The Scriptures. He moved on men of old to document these holy Words of God to us. Picture every Word like a Seed. Within each Word is an invisible and powerful fragrance called joy. Uncommon joy is the hidden essence of each Word of God. When you hear His Words and embrace them, you are receiving holy Seed into the soil of your life. An explosion of unexplainable joy will come forth out of those Seeds like an energizing fragrance. I cannot explain it. It happens every day of my life. The moment I read His Words, changes begin within me.

4. The Holy Spirit Speaks To You Through Events. That's how Israel learned to fear God through the judgments of God on Korah, and others. In the early church the sudden deaths of Ananias and Sapphira were used to bring great fear of God to the early church.

9 Issues The Holy Spirit Will Address In Your Life

1. The Holy Spirit Will Talk To You About Your Sins. "Come now, and let us reason together, saith the Lord: though your sins be as scarlet, they shall be as white as snow; though they be red like crimson, they shall be as wool," (Isaiah 1:18).

2. The Holy Spirit Will Talk To You About Coming Into His Presence. "Come ye, and let us go up to the mountain of the Lord, to the house of the God of Jacob; and He will teach us of His ways, and we will walk in His paths: for out of Zion shall go forth the law, and the word of the Lord from Jerusalem," (Isaiah 2:3).

3.   The Holy Spirit Will Talk To You About Accountability. "So then every one of us shall give account of himself to God," (Romans 14:12).

4.   The Holy Spirit Talks To Children. "Children, obey your parents in the Lord: for this is right. Honour thy father and mother; which is the first commandment with promise; That it may be well with thee, and thou mayest live long on the earth," (Ephesians 6:1-3).

5.   The Holy Spirit Talks To Husbands. "Husbands, love your wives, even as Christ also loved the church, and gave Himself for it; So ought men to love their wives as their own bodies," (Ephesians 5:25, 28).

6.   The Holy Spirit Talks To Wives. "Wives, submit yourselves unto your own husbands, as unto the Lord," (Ephesians 5:22).

7.   The Holy Spirit Will Talk To The Father About You. "Likewise the Spirit also helpeth our infirmities: for we know not what we should pray for as we ought: but the Spirit itself [Himself] maketh intercession for us with groanings which cannot be uttered. And He that searcheth the hearts knoweth what is the mind of the Spirit, because He maketh intercession for the saints according to the will of God," (Romans 8:26-27).

8.   The Holy Spirit Will Talk To You And Confirm That You Belong To God. "The Spirit itself beareth witness with our spirit, that we are the children of God," (Romans 8:16).

9.   The Holy Spirit Will Talk To You About Sowing A Significant Seed Into Others During A Time Of Crisis In Your Life. "And they came, every one whose heart stirred him up, and every one whom his spirit made willing, and they brought the Lord's offering to the work of the tabernacle of the congregation, and for all His service, and for the holy garments," (Exodus 35:21).

It happened to me in a crusade in Kansas. A tall young man sat on the front seat. He would shake his head every time I said something about financial prosperity. It agitated me. But, I kept speaking and sharing the Word of the Lord. Suddenly, The Holy Spirit spoke to my heart. "Empty your entire wallet to him after the service tonight." I turned sick inside. You see, I had just cashed a large check. In fact, I had nine $100 bills and another $200 for a total of $1,100. I had plans and needs. Yet, The Holy Spirit nudged me to empty my entire wallet.

Inside my heart, I replied, "If you will remind me after church, I will do it." Something within me was hoping *he would leave!* I really had no desire whatsoever to give someone like this anything!

After the service, he walked up to me and started a conversation. I said, "The Holy Spirit told me to empty my wallet into you." I handed him $1,100 cash. He looked at it, and kept talking. He shoved it in his pocket and never said a word.

I became upset. When I got back to the hotel, I complained strongly to God. "I just gave him $1,100. He never even spoke a thank you!"

"Why did you do it?"

"Well, You told me to," was my reply.

God indicated that I was to simply shut up! The next day, a phone call came to me worth a minimum of $25,000 to my future. You see, *when The Holy Spirit talks to you about a Seed, He has a Harvest on His mind.*

It happened to the widow of Zarephath. The man of God came to her and talked to her about sowing Seed. It was not his idea at all. The Holy Spirit had instructed him while sitting by the brook, Cherith.

He obeyed *God*.

The widow obeyed *him*.

And, the supply *continued* throughout the days of the famine.

When The Holy Spirit speaks to you, *changes are beginning*.

When The Holy Spirit talks, *joy will flood your heart*.

When The Holy Spirit talks, *obey*.

Always remember, The Holy Spirit loves conversation.

Our Prayer Together...

"Father, thank You for the wonderful gift of my Companion, The Holy Spirit. He is my Mentor, my Teacher, and treasured Friend. Thank You for taking the time to talk to me, converse with me, and reveal instructions to me. Forgive me for the times I have not listened, obeyed and completed Your word. If I have failed to complete any instruction, please speak again to me in such a way I cannot doubt it. Unclutter my life of distractions so that I may hear Your voice and obey You without question. In Jesus' name. Amen."

Uncommon Experiences
Create
Uncommon Men.

-MIKE MURDOCK

≈ 9 ≈

THE HOLY SPIRIT CAN PROVIDE YOU A PRAYER LANGUAGE THAT NOBODY UNDERSTANDS BUT GOD

Your Prayer Language Is A Precious And Important Gift.

While millions have never understood this wonderful and glorious experience, thousands of others are tasting this incredible phenomenon— "praying in the heavenly language." It is quite simple, really.

The Holy Spirit is a Communicator. He even provided animals with sounds to communicate between themselves. The wildest animals on earth communicate to each other!

Relationship is essential in this incredible world of our Creator, The Holy Spirit. He provided every nationality a language of their own. The Spanish have their language. The French have their language. The Germans have their language. The English have their language. The Holy Spirit has a language.

15 Keys You Should Know About Tongues And Your Prayer Language

1. The One Who Gives Languages On Earth Simply Has One Of His Own. Most of us call it The Heavenly Language. "For he that speaketh in an unknown tongue speaketh not unto men, but unto God: for no man understandeth him," (1 Corinthians 14:2).

2. There Are Many Qualities Of This Unknown Tongue That Are Varied, Rewarding And Apply To Different Situations. For example, when The Holy Spirit came on the Day of Pentecost, He provided a language that was unknown only to those who were speaking it! Others *around them* understood because The Holy Spirit was providing an opportunity for the gospel to be heard *in other dialects.* "The multitude came together, and were confounded, because that every man heard them speak in his own language. And they were all amazed and marvelled, saying one to another, Behold are not all these which speak Galilaeans? And how hear we every man in our own tongue, wherein we were born?" (Acts 2:6-8).

Yet, Peter and the others who were speaking "in tongues," did not understand what they were saying. This was *not* the heavenly language, but rather The Holy Spirit using another language or dialect to confirm His presence among them.

3. The Holy Spirit Often Uses Varying Ways To Use "Unknown Tongues" To Impress Unbelievers About A Supernatural God. "Wherefore tongues are for a sign, not to them that believe, but to them that believe not," (1 Corinthians 14:22).

4. The Holy Spirit Is Meticulous And Orderly In How And When Tongues Are Used. Sometimes, when followed by an interpretation, tongues are used to bless the entire church so the people can be edified and blessed. "Wherefore let him that speaketh in an unknown tongue pray that he may interpret," (1 Corinthians 14:13).

5. The Holy Spirit Delights When You Enter Into A Private Time Of Intercession "Through Tongues" For Others. "Likewise the Spirit also helpeth our infirmities: for we know not what we should pray for as we ought: but the Spirit itself [Himself] maketh intercession for us with groanings which cannot be uttered. And He that searcheth the hearts knoweth what is the mind of the Spirit, because He maketh intercession for the saints according to the will of God," (Romans 8:26-27).

6. When You Pray "In Tongues," You Are Building Up Yourself, Your Personal Faith And Confidence In God. Something supernatural occurs. It is indescribable, unexplainable and undeniable. "But ye, beloved, building up yourselves on your most holy faith, *praying in the Holy Ghost,* Keep yourselves in the love of God, looking for the mercy of our Lord Jesus Christ unto eternal life," (Jude 20-21). This is essential for overcomers. You see, *your victories depend on your faith.* Faith is confidence in God. It is *the only way* to bring pleasure to God. "But without faith it is impossible to please Him: for he that cometh to God must believe that He is, and that He is a rewarder of them that diligently seek Him," (Hebrews 11:6).

7. *Recognize* **That Many Times You Do Not Really Know What To Pray About, So It Is Important To Permit The Holy Spirit To Pray Through You.**

8. *Trust* **The Holy Spirit That He Will Not Fail You Or Lead You Into Error.** Remember, He is the Spirit of truth (John 16:13).

9. When You Pray In The Holy Spirit, Trust Him Enough To Avoid Logic And The

Temptation To Understand Everything He Is Doing. He is at work.

I have had unforgettable experiences with my prayer language. I experienced the baptism of The Holy Spirit and "speaking in tongues" at the age of ten. My second dramatic encounter was about the age of fifteen in Beaumont, Texas.

I have always prayed in The Holy Spirit. But, I have never understood the practice of interpreting back in English, my own language, what The Holy Spirit had spoken through me to the Father. One of my beloved mentors, Oral Roberts brought me into a special understanding of this.

I was in a huge conference at the Mabee Center in Tulsa, Oklahoma. After the service one day, Oral Roberts walked over to me and asked me to go with him to one of his offices. There, he began to tell me the secrets behind the remarkable blessings of God on his ministry and work.

"The two keys to everything I have accomplished for God have been Seed-Faith and praying in the Spirit," he explained.

"Mike, God has shown you more about the principle of Seed-Faith than any man I've ever known in my life, but I'd like to tell you about *praying in the Spirit and interpreting back in tongues.*"

Well, this seemed a little strange to me. But, I knew that the hand of God was strong in his life. He has been a remarkable mentor in my life that I value and celebrate. I listened. *Uncommon Experiences Create Uncommon Men.*

He explained that after praying in the Spirit (in tongues), if I would ask The Holy Spirit and be willing to trust Him, He would provide me the interpretation in my own language, English. Then, I could plan and prepare my life according to what The Holy Spirit had been praying through me.

"But," I protested, "What if something comes out of my mouth that is crazy, illogical, and ridiculous?"

"Trust The Holy Spirit," he said gently.

The next morning, I arose at 5:30, my prayer time. I was scheduled to meet with a realtor at 9:30 and purchase an office building in Tulsa. Someone was giving me a ride at 9:00 to the appointment. My manager had been selected and several houses were being purchased for my staff. As I began to pray in the Spirit, suddenly, I began to pray in English. It burst out of my mouth suddenly and unexpectedly: *"This day will not go as you have planned. But, do not fear— it is My Will."*

I felt odd, a little peculiar, but aware that I was moving into a different realm than normal.

At 9:00, my ride appeared. Within 30 minutes, some unexpected things occurred. Statements were made and things happened beyond my control. The purchase of the building was cancelled. The houses for my staff were cancelled. The peace of God came into me to stay in Dallas instead of moving to Tulsa. It was shocking. Yet, as I mentally replayed my prayer time at 5:30 that morning, The Holy Spirit had told me in English that the day "would not go" as I had planned. "What is it then? I will pray with the Spirit, and I will pray with the understanding also," (1 Corinthians 14:15).

It is important for you to keep your prayer language alive and vibrant. "I thank my God, I speak with tongues more than ye all," (1 Corinthians 14:18).

I had two other unusual encounters with my

prayer language in my Secret Place at home. As I was praying fervently in tongues, suddenly I burst out in English these words:

"Expose fraudulent people in my life! Holy Spirit, expose fraudulent people in my life!"

I could hardly believe what was coming from my mouth. Fraudulent people? I did not know any fraudulent people around my life. I trusted everyone close to me explicitly. I have always felt very discerning and that I could "pick up anything wrong." But, The Holy Spirit knew something I did not know. *He knows the hearts of others years before you do.*

I had turned my personal finances over to a long-time friend. I trusted this friend more than any human on earth. Yet, within seven days I discovered this friend had written checks for thousands of dollars unauthorized and without my permission. It was shocking, unsettling and disheartening. But, The Holy Spirit had helped prepare my heart. He was talking to the Father *in my behalf.* When I interpreted in English what He was praying through me (in tongues), it became a spiritual milestone in my memory.

Since then, I have trusted The Holy Spirit to pray anything He desires...knowing that *He wants only that which is good for me.* "No good thing will He withhold from them that walk uprightly," (Psalm 84:11).

A few days later, another uncommon event occurred. As I was praying in the Spirit, suddenly these words burst from my lips:

"Purge my ministry! Holy Spirit, please purge my ministry!"

Purge my ministry? I had no idea what The Holy

Spirit was trying to communicate to the Father. But, I trusted Him. Within seven days or so, someone that I really trusted in my ministry was caught in a sad, terrible and tragic sin. It had been going on periodically for some time. I was too focused on my ministry to notice their erratic behavior. But, The Holy Spirit protected me. He was praying *through me to the Father* that anything unlike Him would be stripped away from our work for God.

Millions have never tapped into this supernatural power. Yet, those who are moving toward a life of total addiction to The Holy Spirit are birthing the most uncommon events of their lifetime.

Before you feed your doubts and misgivings think about this:

You have not been *everywhere*...yet everywhere *continues to exist* without your knowledge.

You do not know *everybody*...yet millions continue to live each day *without your acquaintance.*

You do not know *every* operation of The Holy Spirit...yet millions are tasting the supernatural and uncommon events in their communication with Him...*every day of their life!*

You can, too!

10. *Acknowledge* That You Do Not Know Everything Or Know How To Pray Effective Through Your Own Logic And Mind.

11. *Recognize* The Holy Spirit As Your Earthly Intercessor And Jesus As Your Heavenly Intercessor. Permit them to work through your life.

12. *Ask* For The Prayer Language. "Ye have not, because ye ask not," (James 4:2). Anything you ask in His name, you will receive it according to His will.

13. *Be Willing* To Grow Into The **Relationship.** It may not happen immediately or overnight. Step by step, line upon line, you can begin to build your relationship with The Holy Spirit.

14. *Ask The Holy Spirit* To Draw You **Toward Him.** My father told me this is the greatest and most important prayer someone could ever pray in their whole lifetime. When you get in His presence, you will change. You will behold and see truths you have never seen in your lifetime.

15. *Recognize* And Treasure Any Mentors He Brings Across Your Path To Provide More Revelation About Him.

Walk in the present light you have and more will be provided by the One who created you, The Holy Spirit.

Always remember, The Holy Spirit can provide you a prayer language that nobody understands but God.

Our Prayer Together...

"Precious Holy Spirit, You gave languages to the whole earth to communicate, connect and strengthen relationships. Animals have *sounds*. Humans have *words*. Holy Spirit, You have a special *prayer language* for me to use in my personal prayer life. Teach me, step by step, how to enter into the supernatural prayer life. You are my Intercessor on earth. I celebrate and value each moment in Your presence today. I am willing to be *changed*. I am willing to make new discoveries. Please help me to overcome any erroneous teaching received in my childhood, any prejudices that have come to me through any false teaching. I will pursue You because You are Truth, the Spirit of truth. In Jesus' name. Amen."

❧ 10 ❧

THE HOLY SPIRIT WILL REVEAL SPECIFIC WISDOM YOU REQUIRE FOR LIVING AN OVERCOMING LIFE

Overcomers Are The Only People Rewarded In Eternity.

The Holy Spirit is very reward-conscious. He knows the difference between obedience and disobedience; punishments and rewards. That's why He encouraged us to hear everything He had to say—"He that hath an ear, let him hear what the Spirit saith unto the churches," (Revelation 2:7). "To day if ye will hear His voice, Harden not your heart," (Psalm 95:7-8).

The Holy Spirit always rewards the obedient. He does not necessarily reward good people, smart people, or wealthy people. He rewards *obedient* people.

The Holy Spirit wants you to become an overcomer. "Greater is He that is in you, than he that is in the world," (1 John 4:4).

Jesus taught that The Holy Spirit was the secret of becoming an overcomer. "But ye shall receive power, after that the Holy Ghost is come upon you," (Acts 1:8). The apostle Paul believed that you could be an overcomer. "I can do all things through Christ which strengtheneth me," (Philippians 4:13).

The Holy Spirit gave you The Word of God as a weapon against your enemy. "And the sword of the Spirit, which is the word of God," (Ephesians 6:17).

The Holy Spirit uses The Word to produce the nature of an overcomer within you. "And that from a child thou hast known the holy scriptures, which are able to make thee wise unto salvation through faith which is in Christ Jesus. All scripture is given by inspiration of God, and is profitable for doctrine, for reproof, for correction, for instruction in righteousness: That the man of God may be perfect, throughly furnished unto all good works," (2 Timothy 3:15-17).

The Holy Spirit will reveal to you the secrets of getting along with others. "And in those days, when the number of the disciples was multiplied, there arose a murmuring of the Grecians against the Hebrews, because their widows were neglected in the daily ministration. Then the twelve called the multitude of the disciples unto them, and said, It is not reason that we should leave the word of God, and serve tables. Wherefore, brethren, look ye out among you seven men of honest report, full of the Holy Ghost and wisdom, whom we may appoint over this business. But we will give ourselves continually to prayer, and to the ministry of the word. And the saying pleased the whole multitude," (Acts 6:1-5). "Behold, how good and how pleasant it is for brethren to dwell together in unity! It is like the precious ointment upon the head, that ran down upon the beard, even Aaron's beard: that went down to the skirts of his garments; As the dew of Hermon, and as the dew that descended upon the mountains of Zion:

for there the Lord commanded the blessing, even life for evermore," (Psalm 133:1-3). The Holy Spirit shows us that blessing flows out of the bond of unity.

The Holy Spirit reveals to you the cause of every satanic work around you. "For where envying and strife is, there is confusion and every evil work," (James 3:16).

The Holy Spirit is able to make you an overcomer. You see, He empowered Jesus to overcome satan in the wilderness of temptation (read Matthew 4). The Holy Spirit knows your season of testing (see Luke 4).

The Holy Spirit *knows the weaknesses* of your enemy (Matthew 8). The Holy Spirit knows the *weaponry* you will need to win any battle you are facing.

Oh, you must develop an addiction to The Holy Spirit. Your dependency upon Him is the real reason you can succeed.

You can overcome any bad habit, inner grief and chaotic situation—*through The Holy Spirit.* You can overcome any financial crisis and devastation, bankruptcy and sickness and disease...through the power of The Holy Spirit.

Oh, decide to become an overcomer today!

Always remember, The Holy Spirit will reveal specific Wisdom you require for living an overcoming life.

Our Prayer Together...

"Father, You want me to succeed. I believe that You will assign angels to escort me through any crisis or trial. Thank You for the gift of The Holy Spirit, my Mentor, who will reveal to me step by step how to become an overcomer. In Jesus' name. Amen."

The Anointing You Respect
Is The Anointing
That Increases In Your Life.

-MIKE MURDOCK

≈ 11 ≈

THE HOLY SPIRIT IS THE SOURCE OF THE ANOINTING FOR YOUR LIFE

The Anointing Turns Common Men Into Uncommon Men.

Here Are 18 Facts You Should Know About The Anointing

1. The Anointing Is The Power Of God In A Given Situation. It removes burdens. It destroys yokes that enemies place upon you. The Anointing stops any progress of your enemy immediately.

I have heard several ministers define the Anointing as the "burden-removing, yoke-destroying *power* of God." I think that explains it wonderfully. "And it shall come to pass in that day, that His burden shall be taken away from off thy shoulder, and His yoke from off thy neck, and the yoke shall be destroyed because of the anointing," (Isaiah 10:27).

2. The Anointing Of The Holy Spirit Upon Jesus Enabled Him To Heal The Sick And Cast Out Devils. "How God anointed Jesus of Nazareth with the Holy Ghost and with power: Who went about doing good, and healing all that were oppressed of the devil; for God was with Him," (Acts 10:38).

3. The Anointing Creates Fear In The Heart Of Demonic Spirits. They are subject to that Anointing, the power of God. When that Anointing begins to flow and be released through you, any plan satan has concocted is immediately sabotaged and destroyed. Satan does not fear you, but, rather that *Anointing* which flows through you. That Anointing is the fragrance of The Holy Spirit within you.

4. Jesus Knew That The Anointing Of The Spirit Would Enable The Disciples To Stand Against Anything. "But ye shall receive power, after that the Holy Ghost is come upon you: and ye shall be witnesses unto me both in Jerusalem, and in all Judæa, and in Samaria, and unto the uttermost part of the earth," (Acts 1:8).

That's why Jesus was not shocked when Peter denied Him three times. When the disciples fled at the crucifixion, Jesus was not hopeless. He knew The Holy Spirit. He knew what the Anointing would do within their lives. His instruction to tarry in the Upper Room until The Holy Spirit came was sufficient.

Jesus was not merely trying to make the disciples strong.

He was trying to make them *aware*—of The Holy Spirit to come.

5. The Anointing Is Not Necessarily Energy And Enthusiasm. It is not motion. It is not excitement. It is not noise. It is not exuberance and strength.

6. The Anointing Is The Power Of God To Handle Any Enemy Present In Your Life.

7. The Holy Spirit Imparts A Specific

Anointing Which Abides With You. "But the anointing which ye have received of Him abideth in you," (1 John 2:27). The Holy Spirit is an enablement to surrender your will to God. It is a supernatural power to follow after God with all your heart. That Anointing, enablement, is a gift from the Person within you, The Holy Spirit.

8. **The Holy Spirit Also Imparts Specific Anointings At Particular Moments Of Need.** I have seen it in healing crusades. Suddenly, like a wind, The Holy Spirit moves across an auditorium and eyes suddenly open, ears are unstopped, cancers disappear and the crippled leap from wheel chairs. That specific Anointing is released through the *unity of faith* in that congregation. *Expectation Is The Mountain That Crushes The Pebble Called Satan.* An entire audience can concentrate their faith and focus on Jesus and the power of The Holy Spirit is released in that place against sickness, disease and pain. A hundred miracles can happen simultaneously *when the Anointing is released* through agreement and unity.

9. **It Is Important To Avoid Any Criticism Of Those Who Carry The Anointing Of The Holy Spirit.** "Touch not mine anointed, and do my prophets no harm," (Psalm 105:15). It is a dangerous thing to treat lightly that supernatural Anointing. You see, The Holy Spirit chooses the person He anoints. Men do not choose that Anointing. Crowds cannot decide who carries that Anointing.

10. **The Holy Spirit Selects His Anointed.** He chose Saul to be the first king of Israel. Then, He selected David to follow the kingship of Saul.

11. The Anointing You Respect Is *The Anointing That Grows* In Your Life. When you respect the Anointing for healing, the miracles of healing begin to flow. When you respect an Anointing for financial breakthrough, chains will fall off your life. Ideas and favor will flow like currents, mighty and unstoppable. When you treasure the Anointing for revelation, knowledge will explode within you like a volcano.

12. When You Respect Those Who Are Anointed, Access Will Be Given. (Please read Volume 2 in the series on *The Assignment: The Anointing & The Adversity.* There is much information and more Wisdom Keys regarding the Anointing in this tremendous book.)

The Anointing occurred in different ways throughout the Bible. In the Old Testament, the Anointing came as The Holy Spirit visited men such as Saul. When he would get in the presence of other prophets, he would begin to prophecy *under that Anointing.*

13. The Anointing Upon You Is For Ministry To Others. Jesus felt this Anointing when He asked His disciples who had touched His clothes because virtue had gone out of Him. When His disciples said that many people had been touching Him, He simply said—somebody touched Me with a purpose in mind. Something has been emptied from Me. That is the *purpose* of the Anointing—the power of God is in you to *deliver those in captivity,* and break down prison doors. "The Spirit of the Lord God is upon me; because the Lord hath anointed me to preach good tidings unto the meek; He hath sent me to bind up the brokenhearted, to proclaim liberty to the captives, and the opening of the prison to them that are bound...to comfort all that mourn...to give unto them beauty for ashes, the oil of joy for mourning, the garment of praise for the spirit of heaviness," (Isaiah 61:1-3).

14. You Can Walk In The Anointing Every Moment Of Your Life. As you yield to the leadership of The Holy Spirit, you can begin to live under that Anointing. The Spirit of God is the Source of that power. He qualifies you. He schedules you. He assigns you. He turns you into a deliverer, instead of a captive. The disciples knew this. "Go ye into all the world, and preach the gospel," (Mark 16:15).

15. The Anointing On Your Life Must Be Protected. You see, it is not a frivolous thing to carry the glory and the presence of God around in your life. It is a *holy* thing. You will be held responsible for guarding and nurturing it. Run from frivolity and contention. "But foolish and unlearned questions avoid," (2 Timothy 2:23).

16. There Are Special Times That An Uncommon Anointing Is Placed Upon You For A Specific Reason. After a church service one night, the pastor met me in his office with tears in his eyes. "My brother, you don't really know how God used you tonight," he cried. As he shared with me private and confidential situations existing in his church, I realized that The Holy Spirit had given me words very uncommon that night *for a reason.* This man of God needed an *uncommon* demonstration of the care and compassion of God. He needed a turnaround. So, The Holy Spirit placed an unusual mantle on me for that service...*to solve that specific problem* in that specific church. Heaven came down and chains were broken that night.

17. The Holy Spirit Wants To Anoint You For The Work He Has Called You To Do. So, ask. "Ask, and it shall be given you; seek, and ye shall find; knock, and it shall be opened unto you: For every one that asketh receiveth; and he that seeketh findeth; and to him that knocketh it shall be opened," (Matthew 7:7-8).

18. Treasure The Moment The Holy Spirit Anoints And Does Something Specific And Unique Through You. Do not laugh it off. Do not tease about it. And, do not elaborate and discuss it at length with the wrong people. Humbly thank Him for the privilege of being used to bring healing to the broken.

Always remember, The Holy Spirit is the Source of the Anointing for your life.

Our Prayer Together...

"Heavenly Father, thank You for The Holy Spirit. Thank You for the Anointing, the burden-removing and yoke-destroying power of God. I need Your Anointing and respect those to whom You have given various types of Anointing. I will not criticize any man or woman of God who carries Your presence, Your voice, Your truth, and Your power. *What I respect will come toward me.* I ask You today to send every good and perfect gift that You want me to have. Because I have honored You, obeyed and received Your instructions, I know Your Anointing will flow through me today. Teach me how to protect it from moments of frivolity, carnal conversation, and foolish questioning. In Jesus' name. Amen."

≈ 12 ≈

THE HOLY SPIRIT RAISED JESUS FROM THE DEAD, AFTER HIS CRUCIFIXION

The Holy Spirit Is The Giver Of Life.
"The Spirit of God hath made me, and the breath of the Almighty hath given me life," (Job 33:4).

The Holy Spirit is life. "But the Spirit is life because of righteousness," (Romans 8:10).

The Holy Spirit is also called the Spirit of Christ. "Now if any man have not the Spirit of Christ, he is none of His," (Romans 8:9).

Jesus trusted The Holy Spirit fully. That's why He knew ahead of time that Peter would recover from his devastating moment of denial. He had prayed for Peter. He knew The Holy Spirit would dramatically change this brash, but weak fisherman into a powerful man of God.

Jesus trusted The Holy Spirit to raise Him from the dead. That's one of the reasons He was willing to go through Calvary. The resurrection would follow. "But if the Spirit of Him that raised up Jesus from the dead dwell in you, He that raised up Christ from the dead shall also quicken your mortal bodies by His Spirit that dwelleth in you," (Romans 8:11).

Oh, thank God for the glorious hope of the resurrection! Jesus died, but rose again as an example of what will happen to you and me as we live righteously in Christ.

The Holy Spirit is the enemy of *death.*

The Holy Spirit is the enemy of the *grave.*

The Holy Spirit is the enemy of *hell.*

The disciples could not grasp this, before the death of Christ. After His crucifixion, they returned to their fishing boats, discouraged and demoralized. They were disappointed in everything. They felt hopeless.

But, *The Holy Spirit always finishes what He begins.* On the third day, the stone was rolled away from the tomb. Now, it was not rolled away to let Jesus out. No grave could hold Him. The stone was rolled away—that you and I could see *inside,* that Jesus was risen.

He is *alive!*

He is *alive!*

He is alive!

No other leader in the history of man fulfilled any promise to his disciples that he would return after death. They entered into eternity, dark and gloomy and without hope.

"There is therefore now no condemnation to them which are in Christ Jesus, who walk not after the flesh, but after the Spirit. For the law of the Spirit of life in Christ Jesus hath made me free from the law of sin and death," (Romans 8:1-2).

Your Leader is not a *dead* Leader.

Your Leader is not a *weak* Leader.

Your Leader is not an *ignorant* Leader.

The Holy Spirit raised Jesus from the dead, and He is now seated at the right hand of the Father making intercession for you and me today.

Meanwhile, our Comforter, The Holy Spirit, is making intercession to the Father this very moment.

The best days of your life are *here*.

Get excited! Get ready for the most miraculous season of your whole life as you enter into a special relationship with your Companion and Mentor, The Holy Spirit.

Healing flows through your body today!

Health flows through your very being today!

Always remember this: "For Christ also hath once suffered for sins, the just for the unjust, that He might bring us to God, being put to death in the flesh, but quickened by the Spirit: By which also He went and preached unto the spirits in prison; Which sometime were disobedient, when once the long-suffering of God waited in the days of Noah, while the ark was a preparing, wherein few, that is, eight souls were saved by water," (1 Peter 3:18-20).

Hell is very acquainted with The Holy Spirit. He defeated every plan it concocted; every strategy it had invested in; and raised Jesus from the dead on the third day.

Miracles are being scheduled into your life today! *The Holy Spirit is life.*

Always remember, The Holy Spirit raised Jesus from the dead, after His crucifixion.

Our Prayer Together...

"Precious Father, thank You for reminding us that Jesus is alive and well today. He is our Intercessor in heaven! Thank You for the Spirit of Christ within us today, the precious Holy Spirit, who is birthing the nature of Jesus in us. Yes, we live, yet not we ourselves, but Christ lives in us today...through the presence of The Holy Spirit.

"Cleanse, purify and change anything in me You desire to change. I want to serve You with a whole heart. Mentor me, correct me, and remind me that You will never leave me nor forsake me, because I follow after You. In Jesus' name. Amen."

❧ 13 ❧

THE HOLY SPIRIT DECIDES THE TIMING OF EACH MAJOR TESTING IN YOUR LIFE

━━━▷➌-◉-❸◁━━━

You Will Be Tested.

The Holy Spirit guides you into your wilderness of battle. He did it in the life of Jesus. He will do it in your life as well. "And Jesus being full of the Holy Ghost returned from Jordan, and was led by the Spirit into the wilderness, Being forty days tempted of the devil," (Luke 4:1-2).

The Holy Spirit will test you prior to your promotion. The purpose of your testing is not mere survival. It is to *qualify* you for a promotion, the increase of rewards. The entire earth is motivated by *reward.* God planned it. It is unnatural to pursue decrease. It is normal to pursue increase.

This desire for gain is not satanic. Adam and Eve contained a desire for increase before they ever fell into sin. You see, the first command given to every living creature was to multiply. You have the nature of God within you. The desire to grow is from Him. The desire for increase and multiplication is a characteristic of God. "The thief cometh not, but for to steal, and to kill, and to destroy: I am come that they might have life, and that they might have it more abundantly," (John 10:10).

The Holy Spirit led Jesus into the wilderness. He brought Him into a place of aloneness. *Aloneness always concludes with a battle.*

The battle for your *focus.*

The battle for your *mind.*

The place of testing is always the *place of trust.*

So, The Holy Spirit will always carefully time your season of testing...to qualify you for a season of reward. He does not give you reward for surviving your test. He provides you a test *to qualify you for the rewards* He desires you to experience.

God keeps using everything He has made. He used the *stars* to motivate Abraham's faith for children. He used *water* to turn a marriage into a place of miracles when the wedding party ran out of wine. He used *clay and spittle* to unlock the faith of a blind man. He used a *fish* to give Peter the money he needed to pay his taxes.

He uses satan to qualify you for a blessing.

Everything in your life is a reward or a test. The Holy Spirit always brings you to a place of decision. He leads you to a place of testing.

Here's the wonderful principle: *The Holy Spirit knows your tempter and the questions on the test and will provide every accurate answer necessary.*

The answers are always in The Word of God. Always. When Jesus was being tempted, He didn't cry out for special music so that He could *access* the right frame of mind, or His most "resourceful state." He never said, "I must get back to the synagogue. I had no business coming out here alone." No, Jesus knew the answers. As He began to quote the eternal Word of God, satan became demoralized and paralyzed.

Jesus passed the test and the Anointing began to flow.

Your testing qualifies you for a *promotion.*

Your promotion qualifies you for *rewards.*

Your rewards increase the flow of your *joy.*

The Holy Spirit never makes mistakes.

So, relax in times of testing. He will not let you fail. He knows your enemy. Your enemy always makes mistakes. *Always.*

Your only responsibility is to trust The Holy Spirit. Keep His words in your mind, your mouth and in every conversation.

His words are your weapons. "(For the weapons of our warfare are not carnal, but mighty through God to the pulling down of strong holds;)" (2 Corinthians 10:4).

The Holy Spirit will not permit the test to be too great. "There hath no temptation taken you but such as is common to man: but God is faithful, who will not suffer you to be tempted above that ye are able; but will with the temptation also make a way to escape, that ye may be able to bear it," (1 Corinthians 10:13).

You will experience a double portion of influence and provision as you overcome your present testing. It happened to Job. "And the Lord turned the captivity of Job, when he prayed for his friends: also the Lord gave Job twice as much as he had before," (Job 42:10). That's why it's important for you to be *patient,* knowing that God will answer your prayers. "Behold, we count them happy which endure. Ye have heard of the patience of Job, and have seen the *end* of the Lord; that the Lord is very pitiful, and of tender mercy," (James 5:11).

Always remember, The Holy Spirit decides the timing of each major testing in your life.

Our Prayer Together...

"Heavenly Father, thank You for the *season* of testing. You have decided the timing, my victory, and will empower me through every season. You have already decided that *my enemy will fail,* I will overcome, and You will receive the glory and praise for it. Today, I am patiently praising You for this wonderful season of promotion I am walking toward. In Jesus' name. Amen."

❧ 14 ❧

THE HOLY SPIRIT INTERCEDES FOR YOU CONTINUOUSLY

━━━━━➤◉◄━━━━━

Your Life Is Constantly Covered With Prayer.
You may feel alone. You may feel isolated and even have tormenting thoughts that nobody really cares for you at all. But, the opposite is occurring. The Holy Spirit continuously talks to the Father about your needs and desires.

While you are *asleep*...He prays for you.

While you *work*...He prays for you.

When you feel *doubts*...He prays for you.

You truly are the apple of your Father's eye. "For the Lord's portion is His people; Jacob is the lot of His inheritance. He found Him in a desert land, and in the waste howling wilderness; He led him about, He instructed him, He kept him as the apple of His eye," (Deuteronomy 32:9-10).

The Holy Spirit has committed Himself to your protection. "As an eagle stirreth up her nest, fluttereth over her young, spreadeth abroad her wings, taketh them, beareth them on her wings: So the Lord alone did lead him, and there was no strange god with him," (Deuteronomy 32:11-12).

The Holy Spirit wants you to experience uncommon success and provision. "He made him ride on the high places of the earth, that he might eat the increase of the fields; and He made him to suck honey out of the rock, and oil out of the flinty rock; Butter of kine, and milk of sheep, with fat of lambs, and rams of the breed of Bashan, and goats, with the fat of kidneys of wheat; and thou didst drink the pure blood of the grape," (Deuteronomy 32:13-14). *You and I are limited in our human understanding regarding the gifts and desires of the Father.* That's why our prayers are often ineffective, incomplete and unanswered.

The Holy Spirit has searched out, photographed, inventoried and documented the desires of the Father toward you. "Eye have not seen, nor ear heard, neither have entered into the heart of man, the things which God hath prepared for them that love Him. But God hath revealed them unto us by His Spirit: for the Spirit searcheth all things, yea, the deep things of God," (1 Corinthians 2:9-10).

The Holy Spirit is the only person in the universe that knows the heart of the Father toward you. "For what man knoweth the things of a man, save the spirit of man which is in him? even so the things of God knoweth no man, but the Spirit of God," (1 Corinthians 2:11).

The Holy Spirit is given to you so the desires of the Father can be revealed to you. "Now we have received, not the spirit of the world, but the Spirit which is of God; that we might know the things that are freely given to us of God," (1 Corinthians 2:12).

The Holy Spirit is our committed personal Intercessor every day. "Likewise the Spirit also helpeth our infirmities...but the Spirit itself maketh intercession for us with groanings which cannot be uttered," (Romans 8:26).

The Holy Spirit is in total agreement with the desires and will of the Father for you. "And He that searcheth the hearts knoweth what is the mind of the Spirit, because He maketh intercession for the saints according to the will of God," (Romans 8:27).

The Holy Spirit is passionate about your needs and desires being fulfilled. "But the Spirit itself maketh intercession for us with *groanings which cannot be uttered,"* [emphasis mine] (Romans 8:26).

The Holy Spirit stirs others to become your intercessors also. He did this in Samuel's heart for the people of God. "Moreover as for me, God forbid that I should sin against the Lord in ceasing to pray for you: but I will teach you the good and the right way," (1 Samuel 12:23).

The apostle Paul experienced the same kind of stirring to intercession by The Holy Spirit. His protégé, Timothy, received this word from his mentor. "I thank God, whom I serve from my forefathers with pure conscience, that without ceasing I have remembrance of thee in my prayers night and day," (2 Timothy 1:3).

The Holy Spirit is on earth interceding for you to the Father. "He maketh intercession for the saints according to the will of God," (Romans 8:27). So, there is an incredible and beautiful scenario of intercession occurring 24-hours-a-day, every day of your life.

Jesus is in Heaven praying for you also. "It is Christ that died, yea rather, that is risen again, who is even at the right hand of God, who also maketh intercession for us," (Romans 8:34).

The Holy Spirit will never leave you alone in the storms of your life. Ever. Jesus promised it. "And I will pray the Father, and He shall give you another Comforter, that He may abide with you for ever," (John 14:16).

Your *success* is *not* limited to *your efforts.*

Your *future* is *not* limited by *your personal knowledge.*

Your *victories* are *not* dependent on your own personal abilities *alone.*

The Holy Spirit and Jesus are your personal intercessors throughout every trial and difficult place of your life. That's why the apostle Paul could shout with joy and thanksgiving in the midst of the most difficult, cold, damp prison experiences: "Who shall separate us from the love of Christ? shall tribulation, or distress, or persecution, or famine, or nakedness, or peril, or sword? Nay in all these things we are more than conquerors through Him that loved us. For I am persuaded, that neither death, nor life, nor angels, nor principalities, nor powers, nor things present, nor things to come, Nor height, nor depth, nor any other creature, shall be able to separate us from the love of God, which is in Christ Jesus our Lord," (Romans 8:35, 37-39).

Your natural man (the self-life) rejects continuously the things of The Holy Spirit. "But the natural man receiveth not the things of the Spirit of God: for they are foolishness unto him: neither can he know them, because they are spiritually discerned," (1 Corinthians 2:14).

Humans simply do not know how to pray. "For we know not what we should pray for as we ought," (Romans 8:26).

Always remember, The Holy Spirit intercedes for you continuously.

Our Prayer Together...

"Precious Father, thank You for hearing my prayers today. You always respond to the cries of my heart. Thank You most of all for hearing the intercessions of my precious Comforter, The Holy Spirit, every day of my life. Thank You for receiving the prayers of Jesus, the One who died for me. Today, I will enthusiastically rest in peace and joy every moment because You will answer the prayers of those who are interceding for me. I am so thankful also, Father, that You are stirring other men and women of God to call my name before Your throne. You are imparting faith and have promised total victory. I accept it, in Jesus' name. Amen."

The Evidence
Of God's Presence
Far Outweighs The Proof
Of His Absence.

-MIKE MURDOCK

≈ 15 ≈

THE HOLY SPIRIT IS KEENLY AWARE OF THE SMALLEST DETAILS OF YOUR LIFE

The Holy Spirit Notices Everything.

Your tears affect The Holy Spirit. When others fail to see your tears, He has recorded them. "Thou tellest my wanderings: put thou my tears into thy bottle: are they not in thy book?" (Psalm 56:8). "The sacrifices of God are a broken spirit: a broken and a contrite heart, O God, thou wilt not despise," (Psalm 51:17).

Your tears bring His commitment to perform for you. "I will cry unto God most high; unto God that performeth all things for me," (Psalm 57:2).

Every sparrow that falls to the ground receives the attention of God. "Are not five sparrows sold for two farthings, and not one of them is forgotten before God?...Fear not therefore: ye are of more value than many sparrows," (Luke 12:6-7).

The hairs of your head are even numbered by God. "But even the very hairs of your head are all numbered," (Luke 12:7).

Your offerings receive the attention of God, regardless of their size. "And Jesus sat over against the treasury, and beheld how the people cast money into the treasury: and many that were rich cast in much. And there came a certain poor widow, and she threw in two mites, which make a farthing. And He called unto Him His disciples, and saith unto them, Verily I say unto you, That this poor widow hath cast more in, than all they which have cast into the treasury: For all they did cast in of their abundance; but she of her want did cast in all that she had, even all her living," (Mark 12:41-44).

The Holy Spirit knows the very moment that financial crisis occurs in your personal life. The widow of Zarephath discovered this. Elijah was being fed miraculously by a raven by the brook, Cherith (1 Kings 17). The day that the widow was on her very last meal, God stopped the raven from bringing food to Elijah. That day signaled a miraculous change. God sent Elijah to the widow *to unlock her faith*. The Bible says that she, her family and the man of God continued to eat throughout the famine. The Holy Spirit knew *the very day* she was scheduled to eat her last meal on earth.

Oh, our God is glorious and wonderful! *Nothing escapes His attention.* While the ungodly may experience anger or even fear because of the continuous eyes of God upon them, those who are obedient *delight* in the constant surveillance of their circumstances.

Somebody is *watching* out for you.

Somebody is *recognizing* your efforts.

Somebody is *listening* to your praise today.

Somebody is *scheduling your supply* even while you are looking at your losses.

Somebody is *planning your recovery* tomorrow

while you are discussing your failures from yesterday.

The Holy Spirit.

*The Holy Spirit is ever working in your behalf,
because of the love of the Father for your life.* "No good
thing will He withhold from them that walk
uprightly," (Psalm 84:11).

*The Holy Spirit knows specifically what you need
during times of mental anguish and confusion.* That's
why He sent Philip to discuss the perplexities of the
Ethiopian eunuch in his own chariot. "Then the Spirit
said unto Philip, Go near, and join thyself to this
chariot. And Philip ran thither to him, and heard him
read the prophet Esaias, and said, Understandest
thou what thou readest? And he said, How can I,
except some man should guide me? And he desired
Philip that he would come up and sit with him," (Acts
8:29-31).

Your *confusion* does not *embarrass* Him.

Your *ignorance* does not *agitate* Him.

Your *anger* does not *intimidate* Him.

The Holy Spirit is keenly aware of the emotional
currents you are experiencing...every single moment.

Your family may be too busy to notice.

Your best friend may feel too baffled to help.

But, the Comforter, who walks beside you, is *continuously* advising you, protecting you and scheduling
miraculous events to keep you focused on your
Assignment and the dreams of God for your life.

*David understood the awesome attentiveness of
The Holy Spirit.* "O Lord, Thou hast searched me, and
known me. Thou knowest my downsitting and mine
uprising, Thou understandest my thought afar off.
Thou compassest my path and my lying down, and art

acquainted with all my ways. For there is not a word in my tongue, but, lo, O Lord, Thou knowest it altogether. Thou hast beset me behind and before, and laid Thine hand upon me," (Psalm 139:1-5).

Always remember, The Holy Spirit is keenly aware of the smallest details of your life.

Our Prayer Together...
"Heavenly Father, Your eyes run to and fro upon the earth to find someone to show Yourself mighty toward. I am here today, thankful and grateful for every moment of Your attention. It is big and important to me. Thank You for reminding me that every attack of satan has been noted and that my deliverance is being scheduled...even while I talk to You today.

"I do not know my future, but You do.

"I do not know how to satisfy the needs of my own life—but You do.

"Holy Spirit, I relax in Your precious arms today. You will not leave me without victory. I will walk thankfully, appreciative and full of joy because You are aware of every single trial, difficulty and victory I am needing. In Jesus' name. Amen."

≈ 16 ≈
THE HOLY SPIRIT IS DELIGHTED WHEN YOU SING TO HIM

———————▶>-0-◀<———————

Singing Is Very Important To The Holy Spirit.

The Holy Spirit sings over you as well. "The Lord thy God in the midst of thee is mighty; He will save, He will rejoice over thee with joy; He will rest in His love, *He will joy over thee with singing,*" [emphasis mine] (Zephaniah 3:17).

Many people cannot imagine our God singing. But, He does! I can picture this so clearly in my heart. The Holy Spirit is like a mother leaning over the bed of her small child and singing, "Sleep, my precious baby! Sleep, precious love of my life. I will watch over you and protect you, until the day that follows this night."

15 Facts You Should Know About Singing

1. The Holy Spirit Wants You To Sing When You Enter His Presence. "Come before His presence with singing," (Psalm 100:2).

Sounds are wonderful to The Holy Spirit! Listen to the birds today as they sing out in wonderment! Listen to the sounds of animals, the wind blowing through the trees and even the wonderful love sounds of those family members close to you. Singing is an essential part of this world. That's why The Holy Spirit wants you to be aware of His fervent desire to hear you sing to Him!

2.   Sing To Him Specifically, Not Just To People. I have written over 5,000 songs throughout my lifetime. Yet, the songs I love to sing the most are the songs to The Holy Spirit. I call them, *Love Songs to The Holy Spirit.* Hundreds of songs have been birthed in my heart since I fell in love with The Holy Spirit on July 13, 1994.

3.   Sing From Your Heart, Not Your Mind. He does not need fancy words, unusual philosophy or beautiful sounds. He simply wants you to open your heart and let the "love sounds" flow from you (1 Corinthians 13).

4.   Sing In Your Prayer Language, Too. The apostle Paul understood the incredible power of singing. "I will sing with the Spirit, and I will sing with the understanding also," (1 Corinthians 14:15). "And at midnight Paul and Silas prayed, and sang praises unto God," (Acts 16:25).

5.   The Holy Spirit Wants You To Sing Together With Other Saints. "Let the word of Christ dwell in you richly in all wisdom; teaching and admonishing one another in psalms and hymns and spiritual songs, singing with grace in your hearts to the Lord," (Colossians 3:16).

6.   When You Sing To The Holy Spirit, Evil Spirits Will Leave. King Saul discovered this under the anointed music ministry of David. In fact, the music of David refreshed Saul. "And it came to pass, when the evil spirit from God was upon Saul, that David took an harp, and played with his hand: so Saul was refreshed, and was well, and the evil spirit departed from him," (1 Samuel 16:23).

That's why I placed 24 speakers on the trees in my seven-acre yard. I can't tell you how wonderful it is to walk across my yard, hearing these songs to The Holy Spirit. Also, stereo speakers have been installed throughout the rooms of my home, playing songs to The Holy Spirit continuously. Words cannot describe the effect it has in your heart and mind. In fact, recently when some of my CD's (compact discs) were damaged, it seemed like death replaced life around my house! *The Holy Spirit comes when He is celebrated.*

Invest in an excellent, quality stereo and make music a major part of every day. It is worth every penny. Your *mind* will respond. Your *heart* will find new fire. Your *body* will receive a surging of new energy and vitality. Most of all, The Holy Spirit will manifest His presence.

7. Singers Were An Essential Part Of Battles In The Old Testament. Listen to the conduct of Jehoshaphat. "When he had consulted with the people, he appointed singers unto the Lord, and that should praise the beauty of holiness, as they went out before the army, and to say, Praise the Lord; for His mercy endureth for ever," (2 Chronicles 20:21).

8. Singers Were Often The Reason For Victories Against The Enemies Of God. "And when they began to sing and to praise, the Lord set ambushments against the children of Ammon, Moab, and mount Seir, which were come against Judah; and they were smitten," (2 Chronicles 20:22).

Your singing to The Holy Spirit *will create an atmosphere of thanksgiving.*

Your singing will greatly *influence your focus.*

Your singing can dispel e*very demonic influence*

designed to distract you.

Your singing will arouse the energy and passion of your own body to focus on your Creator.

Your singing is an act of obedience to The Holy Spirit (Psalm 100:2).

9.   Your Singing Can Affect Nature Itself. Read again the incredible story of Paul and Silas in prison. Everything was going against them. They had been beaten. They were alone and in incredible pain. But, they understood the *Weapon of Singing.* "And at midnight Paul and Silas prayed, and sang praises unto God: and the prisoners heard them.   And suddenly there was a great earthquake, so that the foundations of the prison were shaken: and immediately all the doors were opened, and every one's bands were loosed," (Acts 16:25-26).   The foundations were destroyed...*as they began to sing.*

10. Singing   Can   Make   Your   Enemy Demoralized, Discouraged And Decide To Move Away From You. Paul watched this happen when he and Silas sang in the prison.   "And the keeper of the prison awaking out of his sleep, and seeing the prison doors open, he drew out his sword, and would have killed himself, supposing that the prisoners had been fled," (Acts 16:27).

11.   Your Singing May Be The Turning Point In Someone's Personal Salvation. It happened for the jailer when Paul and Silas sang.   "Then he called for a light, and sprang in, and came trembling, and fell down before Paul and Silas, And brought them out, and said, Sirs, what must I do to be saved?" (Acts 16:29-30).

12. Moses, The Great Leader, Understood

The Heart Of God About Singing. After Israel saw Pharaoh's army destroyed, they sang. "Then sang Moses and the children of Israel this song unto the Lord, and spake, saying, I will sing unto the Lord, for He hath triumphed gloriously: the horse and his rider hath He thrown into the sea," (Exodus 15:1).

13. Deborah, The Great Prophetess, Understood How To Express Appreciation Of God Through Singing. After the defeat of Sisera and Jabin, she honored the Lord. "Then sang Deborah and Barak...Praise ye the Lord for the avenging of Israel, when the people willingly offered themselves. Hear, O ye kings; give ear, O ye princes; I, even I, will sing unto the Lord; I will sing praise to the Lord God of Israel," (Judges 5:1-3).

14. Great Healing Ministries Emphasize Singing. Sometimes, I have sat for two to three hours before the miracles and healings began. Songs that honored The Holy Spirit and the greatness of God seemed to unlock faith into the atmosphere. He always comes when He is celebrated and honored. You see, He instructed us how to approach Him—come with singing (Psalm 100:2).

15. Singing Can Change Everything Around Your Life. *Everything.* So, begin this very moment. Close this book and begin to sing *aloud* to The Holy Spirit. Your words may be simple, but they will become powerful.

"I love You, Holy Spirit!
I love You, Holy Spirit!
I love You, Holy Spirit!
You are good, so good to me!"

So, you and I can learn from the champions.

Those who have conquered in battle have discerned the hidden and mysterious power of singing. You must do it in your own life today! "Saying, I will declare Thy name unto my brethren, in the midst of the church will I sing praise unto Thee," (Hebrews 2:12).

Always remember, The Holy Spirit is delighted when you sing to Him.

Our Prayer Together...

"Father, thank You for revealing the Weapon of Singing to my life. I will sing...when things go wrong or right. I will sing *regardless of my circumstances.* I will sing for the purpose of *honoring You* and obeying You! I will sing *songs of remembrance,* because I remember every blessing You have given me over the years! I will sing *continuously*, knowing that as I sing, angels come and minister to me! I will sing with *victory*, knowing that demonic spirits are becoming fragmented and confused when they hear my words. I will sing, knowing that my mouth is my *Deliverer!* I will teach *my children* to sing to You! I will have songs played in my home, in my car and on my job continuously...to honor Your presence! *Thank You for singing to me* over my life! In Jesus' name. Amen."

≈ 17 ≈

THE HOLY SPIRIT IS YOUR ONLY SOURCE OF TRUE JOY ON EARTH

————◆————

True Success Is The Presence Of Joy.

The presence of The Holy Spirit brings joy. "In thy presence is fulness of joy; at thy right hand there are pleasures for evermore," (Psalm 16:11).

The fruit of the Spirit is joy. "But the fruit of the Spirit is love, *joy,* peace, longsuffering, gentleness, goodness, faith, Meekness, temperance: against such there is no law," (Galatians 5:22-23).

Wisdom increases your joy. "Happy is the man that findeth wisdom, and the man that getteth understanding," (Proverbs 3:13).

The Holy Spirit is the Spirit of Wisdom! "And the Spirit of the Lord shall rest upon him, the Spirit of wisdom and understanding, the Spirit of counsel and might, the Spirit of knowledge and of the fear of the Lord," (Isaiah 11:2).

Joy is much different than enthusiasm and energy. Many times you and I will experience the completion of a great project or task and we experience enthusiasm. Unfortunately, it normally lasts just a few minutes then our focus changes to another problem to conquer. So, our enthusiasm is often based on the circumstances of our life and our achievements. Nothing is sadder than to watch someone build their whole life around human achievement in pursuit of joy.

Some pursue money thinking it will produce joy. Yet, the richest people on earth sometimes seem to be the most sorrowful in many circumstances. The famous have been known to commit suicide, even though millions were in their bank accounts.

Some depend on their loved ones to create an atmosphere of happiness. The husband blames the wife for his unhappiness. The wife sometimes blames her husband for her unhappiness. The children blame the parents and their strict rules for their personal loss of joy and enthusiasm. The unemployed blame the economy for their lack of joy.

Most people think their joy comes from 1) people, 2) promotion, 3) progress, 4) power or 5) possessions.

The wise person discovers the truth. The Holy Spirit creates joy within you every moment that He is pleasured.

When you are pleasuring Him through total obedience, you will feel what He is feeling.

When you grieve Him and bring Him sorrow, you will feel what He is feeling.

The apostle Paul gave us an incredible photograph: "For the kingdom of God is not meat and drink; but righteousness, and peace, and joy in the Holy Ghost," (Romans 14:17).

The Holy Spirit will give you joy in the midst of your most difficult and fiery trial. The apostles discovered this. After they were beaten, they kept their joy. "And when they had called the apostles, and beaten them, they commanded that they should not speak in the name of Jesus, and let them go. And they departed from the presence of the council, rejoicing that they were counted worthy to suffer shame for His name," (Acts 5:40-41).

The joy of The Holy Spirit enables you to keep doing your Assignment in the midst of threats. "And daily in the temple, and in every house, they ceased not to teach and preach Jesus Christ," (Acts 5:42).

When The Holy Spirit controls your life, your words will become catalysts for blessing. "A man hath joy by the answer of his mouth: and a word spoken in due season, how good is it!" (Proverbs 15:23).

Always remember, The Holy Spirit is your only Source of true joy on earth.

Our Prayer Together...

"Holy Spirit, keeping Your presence is the most important thing in the world to me. Only Your presence, nothing else, matters! I am satisfied, at peace and victorious. Thank You for reminding me of the emptiness of things, the futility of pleasuring people and the joy You always produce in my life. In Jesus' name. Amen."

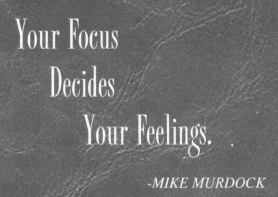

Your Focus
Decides
Your Feelings.

-MIKE MURDOCK

⟐ 18 ⟐
THE HOLY SPIRIT IS YOUR ONLY SOURCE OF TRUE PEACE

Peace Is The Absence Of Inner Conflict.

Inner battle is devastating. Sometimes, our conscience is at war against things we have done. Our focus on *things* greatly influences our emotions. If you analyze, evaluate, and continually think about injustices done to you, your heart will become chaotic. Your mind will become fragmented. Your attitude will become critical.

The Holy Spirit solves every inner turmoil.

The fruit of The Holy Spirit is peace. "But the fruit of the Spirit is love, joy, *peace,* longsuffering, gentleness, goodness, faith, Meekness, temperance: against such there is no law," (Galatians 5:22-23).

You see, *His presence brings peace.* When you obey His instructions, a calmness will enter your spirit. The greatest warfare of your life is The Holy Spirit versus your flesh and self. "For the flesh lusteth against the Spirit, and the Spirit against the flesh: and these are contrary the one to the other: so that ye cannot do the things that ye would," (Galatians 5:17).

When you permit the leadership of The Holy Spirit in your life, you will enter the most remarkable and unforgettable season of calm and inner peace you could imagine.

Man cannot give this peace.

Popularity does not create this kind of peace.

Wealth cannot produce this peace.

Counselors cannot produce this kind of peace.

A *loving mate* does not produce this kind of peace.

Uncommon peace is a gift from an uncommon God. "And the peace of God, which passeth all understanding, shall keep your hearts and minds through Christ Jesus," (Philippians 4:7).

When you focus on The Holy Spirit, your mind begins to grow and become the mind of Christ. "For to be carnally minded is death; but to be spiritually minded is life and peace," (Romans 8:6).

When The Holy Spirit becomes your focus, the storm begins to settle in your mind. You enter into the rest He promised. "This is the rest wherewith ye may cause the weary to rest; and this is the refreshing," (Isaiah 28:12).

The Holy Spirit must become your focus before you ever experience total and continuous peace. "Thou wilt keep him in perfect peace, whose mind is stayed on Thee: because he trusteth in Thee," (Isaiah 26:3).

There Are 3 Ways The Holy Spirit Affects Your Life

1. The Holy Spirit Will Give You Discernment Regarding Your Friendships. Some are contentious. Their fault-finding words create a climate of conflict, anger and cynicism. "From such turn away," (2 Timothy 3:5). Mark people who carry a spirit of debate and strife. When The Holy Spirit is in leadership, you will discern such people quickly. "But foolish and unlearned questions avoid, knowing that they do gender strifes," (2 Timothy 2:23).

2. The Holy Spirit Increases Your Patience Which Always Brings Peace In A Social Setting As Well. "And the servant of the Lord must not strive; but be gentle unto all men, apt to teach, patient," (2 Timothy 2:24). *Unfortunately, most of us blame everyone around us for the climate of battle.* However, battle requires two or more. If you refuse to fight, the war cannot continue. "Where no wood is, there the fire goeth out: so where there is no talebearer, the strife ceaseth. As coals are to burning coals, and wood to fire; so is a contentious man to kindle strife," (Proverbs 26:20-21).

3. The Holy Spirit Will Give You The Courage And Strength To Withdraw From The Company Of Foolish People. This increases your peace. "Go from the presence of a foolish man, when thou perceivest not in him the lips of knowledge," (Proverbs 14:7).

After a service one night, I was so happy. Many had come to Christ. A good number had been healed. Everything was so peaceful. When several of us arrived at the restaurant, a staff person from the local church began to complain to the waitress. A spot or something was on their glass. Within a few moments, everyone circulated their experiences of "roaches in food" and other unhappy and unfortunate experiences with restaurants during their lifetime. In less than thirty minutes we went from a glorious move of The Holy Spirit, to pessimism and despondency.

It came through one person.

You are a Door or a Wall. You can become a Wall against discouragement, cynicism and pessimism. Or, you can be a Door for others to walk through and continue in the presence of God.

Sometimes, it is wonderful to be a Door that the presence of God can walk through.

But it is sometimes necessary to become a Wall against things that are unholy, unrighteous and that bring unhappiness.

The Word of God is the instrument of peace for The Holy Spirit to use. "Great peace have they which love Thy law: and nothing shall offend them," (Psalm 119:165). *When The Word of God is sown continuously in your heart, it grows a Harvest of peace.*

When someone approaches me in great emotional havoc and disturbance, I know that The Word of God is not dominating their life. They discuss their battles instead of the One who is fighting for them.

They discuss their warfare, instead of the promise of victory.

They discuss their doubts, instead of their faith in God.

Their focus is their enemy, instead of their Comforter.

If The Word of God were dominating their mouth, it would dominate their mind.

If The Word of God were dominating their mind, it would influence their conduct and behavior.

You must embrace The Word of God as the most effective instrument for change. That's why Paul wrote Timothy, "All scripture is given by inspiration of God, and is profitable for doctrine, for reproof, for correction, for instruction in righteousness: That the man of God may be perfect, throughly furnished unto all good works," (2 Timothy 3:16-17).

The Holy Spirit inspired the Scriptures.

The Holy Spirit affects your words.

The Holy Spirit uses The Word of God to bring peace into your heart. Don't throw it away. Don't treat it lightly.

Here Are 4 Keys To Creating A Peaceful Climate

1. Recognize That Conflict Is The Trap Of Distraction. Satan uses conflict to break your focus on your Assignment. Have you ever wondered, after an argument with someone, why they have focused on such trivia? It didn't make sense. Any sense at all. Some have forfeited a twenty year friendship of marriage, because of one sentence spoken in a day. That's demonic. It's satanic. It's not even logical. The purpose was to break your focus on things that are good.

That's why the apostle Paul wrote to the church at Philippi, "And the peace of God, which passeth all understanding, shall keep your hearts and minds through Christ Jesus...whatsoever things are true... honest... just...pure...lovely...of good report...think on these things," (Philippians 4:7-8).

2. You Determine Your Own Focus. Nobody else can. You can complain. You can blame others. But, you are responsible for what you give your attention to.

3. Your Focus Is Creating Your Feelings. Whatever you are feeling is produced by your focus. Your focus is your personal decision. Stop, take time to change your focus.

4. Pay Any Price To Protect Your Focus

And Keep It On Right Things. "And if thy hand offend thee, cut it off: it is better for thee to enter into life maimed, than having two hands to go into hell, into the fire that never shall be quenched...And if thine eye offend thee, pluck it out: it is better for thee to enter into the kingdom of God with one eye, than having two eyes to be cast into hell fire," (Mark 9:43, 47). "Thou wilt keep him in perfect peace, whose mind is stayed on Thee," (Isaiah 26:3).

Always remember, The Holy Spirit is your only Source of true peace.

Our Prayer Together...

"Father, thank You for the promise of peace. The world is in battle. Every day is an emotional war. Everything around me seems designed to break my focus and create distraction. But, Your Word is a lamp unto my feet and a light unto my path. Because I love Thy Word, my peace is great. Holy Spirit, You are the true Source of peace. You are the Spirit of peace, and we embrace You today. Your words matter to me. Thank You for The Word of God, the Instrument of Peace, that You have given to me. It drives out darkness and brings me into a place of rest. In Jesus' name. Amen."

❦ 19 ❦

THE HOLY SPIRIT CAN ELIMINATE ALL FEAR OF MAN

Fear Is Tormenting.

Fear increases the size of your enemy *mentally.* Fear causes your hope to shrivel and die. Fear is a devastating tool of satan that has robbed millions of a victorious life.

The Israelites' journey toward Canaan has been told countless times. They left Egypt with a flurry of miracles. God had used painful and devastating situations to persuade Pharaoh. His determination to keep the Israelites in Egypt withered under the awesome power of God. Moses was a remarkable leader. His patience is legendary. The Israelites hated the days of Egyptian slavery.

At last, they were headed toward Canaan, the Land of Promise. The grapes were huge. The land was luscious. The supply was limitless.

But, there were giants in their Land of Promise.

Twelve spies were chosen to review and evaluate the land of Canaan. Ten returned full of doubt and unbelief. Two returned with great faith—Joshua and Caleb. However, when the ten spies began to talk about the size of the giants and said, "We are like grasshoppers in their sight," the hope of the Israelites died within them.

They wept all night. The faith of the two spies was totally disregarded. The Israelites forfeited the incredible promised land of Canaan.

Forty more years of wandering occurred, not because of the giants, but because of their *fear* of the giants.

Giants *cannot* destroy you.

Your fear of your giants can destroy you.

Imagine being one of the children of the Israelites. Your ear is listening at the campfire of your parents while they discuss their fear of the giants— people they had never even yet seen. They have toiled and labored as slaves. Now, they seem to have forgotten those days.

Their pain of the past is gone.

They have forgotten the tears of slavery.

Their focus is the giants—their obstacles in the Land of Promise.

What a picture of life! God has given us many promises of miracles, Harvests and supernatural blessings. Yet, the giants are always there that *require conquering*.

Champions are not crowned for *desiring* to be champions.

Champions are crowned *after* they defeat *an enemy*.

You have no right to a victory for which you have not *fought*.

You do not have a right to anything you have not *pursued*.

Warfare is necessary for your victory.

Victory qualifies you for rewards.

Overcomers are the only people The Holy Spirit

will reward in eternity. "He that overcometh, the same shall be clothed in white raiment; and I will not blot out his name out of the book of life, but I will confess his name before My Father, and before His angels," (Revelation 3:5).

"Him that overcometh will I make a pillar in the temple of My God, and he shall go no more out: and I will write upon him the name of My God, and the name of the city of My God, which is new Jerusalem, which cometh down out of heaven from My God: and I will write upon him My new name," (Revelation 3:12).

"To him that overcometh will I grant to sit with Me in My throne, even as I also overcame, and am set down with My Father in His throne," (Revelation 3:21).

Fear torments. "Fear hath torment," (1 John 4:18).

Love is an enemy of fear. When love fills your heart, fear has no place in your life. "There is no fear in love; but perfect love casteth out fear: because fear hath torment. He that feareth is not made perfect in love," (1 John 4:18).

The fruit of The Holy Spirit is love. "But the fruit of the Spirit is love, joy, peace, longsuffering, gentleness, goodness, faith," (Galatians 5:22).

So, your life in the Spirit will cause fear to dissolve and be dispelled from your life.

The disciples lost their fears after the coming of The Holy Spirit. Peter denied the Lord. Thomas doubted Him. Judas betrayed Him and committed suicide. Every disciple fled and ran away during the crucifixion. The disciples were embarrassed, humiliated, shamed and confused.

Think about it. When the maiden at the home of the high priest questioned Peter, he crumbled. Perhaps, this was the experience Jesus referred to earlier when He spoke to Peter. "Simon, Simon, behold, satan hath desired to have you, that he may sift you as wheat: But I have prayed for thee, that thy faith fail not: and when thou art converted, strengthen thy brethren," (Luke 22:31-32). Jesus warned him of an enemy. He saw satan setting the trap.

Anything close to Jesus receives attack.

Yet, Jesus truly believed that Peter would overcome every pitfall of satan. He anticipated the success of Peter. "When thou art converted." Jesus did not say..."if." He said..."when."

Then, He provided Peter *another focus.* "Strengthen your brethren." What was He saying?

Stop your introspection.

Don't over-analyze the attack of satan against you.

Don't boast to everybody about your great ability to overcome.

Now, *focus on others.* Many are experiencing fear, unbelief and weakness like yourself. Focus on *their overcoming.*

This is the incredible work of The Holy Spirit. "For God hath not given us the spirit of fear; but of power, and of love, and of a sound mind," (2 Timothy 1:7).

The disciples did not even fear while they experienced beatings. They rejoiced and were happy that they were considered worthy to suffer for the name of Jesus. "When they had called the apostles, and beaten them, they commanded that they should not speak in the name of Jesus, and let them go. And they departed from the presence of the council, rejoicing that they were counted worthy to suffer shame for His name," (Acts 5:40-41).

The disciples intensified their obedience and evangelism after the beatings. "And daily in the temple, and in every house, they ceased not to teach and preach Jesus Christ," (Acts 5:42).

Dreams have been dashed on the Rocks of Fear for hundreds of years. Champions carrying the Seeds of Greatness within them have lost their grip on incredible goals and dreams...because of fear.

I heard someone say that a baby is born with two basic fears. But, by the time the child is 20 years old, over 172,000 fears have been documented.

14 Facts You Should Know About Fear

Fear changes your *focus*.

Fear *weakens your resolve*, determination and will power.

Fear breaks the Golden Connection of choice friendships.

Fear has crushed the hopes of a young man and woman about to be married.

Fear has sabotaged a million promotions.

Fear prevents you from making important changes in your life.

Fear wears various disguises. It wraps itself in the Robe of Reality, Honesty, Caution and Logic.

Fear is a more deceptive enemy than satan.

Fear is *within* you.

Fear stops you from *reaching*—thinking that rejection will await.

Fear stops you from *asking* for forgiveness—afraid that mercy will not be offered.

Fear stops you from *admitting* your guilt and that you are wrong—afraid that grace will not be returned.

The Holy Spirit is an enemy to fear. The Holy Spirit is the One who sustained Jesus in the Garden of Gethsemane when He prayed concerning "the cup of suffering."

The fear of man can stop physical healings from occurring in your body. Look at the blind man. He cried out, "Jesus, Thou son of David, have mercy on me." The crowd around him told him to hold his peace (Mark 10:48).

But, he refused to fear the opposition of men around him. And, he received his miracle.

Millions have surrendered to their fears...while their heart dreams for a miracle.

Don't let this happen to you today.

Come into His presence. Reach out toward The Holy Spirit. Ask Him to dispel every ounce of fear within you. Begin to thank Jesus for paying the price, making you an overcomer and interceding for you before the Father.

Somebody is fighting hell for you today.

Somebody will defeat fear for you today.

That Somebody is The Holy Spirit.

Many fears exist: the fear of loss...failure...poverty...false accusation...sickness and disease...cancer...rejection. But, you have a Friend, the Comforter, The Holy Spirit.

Always remember, The Holy Spirit can eliminate all fear of man.

Our Prayer Together...

"Heavenly Father, I boldly come to You in the Name of Jesus. You have commanded me to ask largely of You, anything regarding the work of Your hands. Today, I ask You for holy boldness like the disciples experienced during the days of the outpouring of The Holy Spirit. Father, I reject fear. I receive faith. Your love fills my heart today. I know You love me. You know that I love You. So, I walk as an overcomer today.

"In the Name of Jesus, I agree with Your Word that fear cannot remain in me. I open the door of my heart to faith, confidence, and full trust in You. You will not disappoint me. Thank You for the promise of victory; You are my victorious healing and Best Friend. In Jesus' name. Amen."

What Happens
In Your Mind
Will Happen
In Time.

-MIKE MURDOCK

≈ 20 ≈

THE HOLY SPIRIT CAN REVEAL FUTURE EVENTS TO YOU BEFORE THEY EVEN HAPPEN

The Holy Spirit Sees Far Ahead.

He will show you events before they ever occur. Jesus promised this would happen. "He will shew you things to come," (John 16:13).

The Holy Spirit is the Spirit of prophecy. "For the prophecy came not in old time by the will of man: but holy men of God spake as they were moved by the Holy Ghost," (2 Peter 1:21).

The Holy Spirit spoke ahead of time about scoffers making light of the coming of Christ in the last days. "That ye may be mindful of the words which were spoken before by the holy prophets, and of the commandment of us the apostles of the Lord and Saviour: Knowing this first, that there shall come in the last days scoffers, walking after their own lusts, And saying, Where is the promise of His coming?" (2 Peter 3:2-4).

The Holy Spirit gave the great prophet, Samuel, photographs of future events. "Now the Lord had told Samuel in his ear a day before Saul came, saying, To morrow about this time I will send thee a man out of the land of Benjamin, and thou shalt anoint him to be captain over My people Israel, that he may save My people out of the hand of the Philistines," (1 Samuel 9:15-16).

The Holy Spirit came upon David when Samuel anointed him. "Then Samuel took the horn of oil, and anointed him in the midst of his brethren: and the Spirit of the Lord came upon David from that day forward," (1 Samuel 16:13).

The Holy Spirit inspires, anoints and qualifies men and women to prophecy to others as well. "For to one is given by the Spirit the word of wisdom; to another the word of knowledge by the same Spirit; To another the working of miracles; to another prophecy; to another discerning of spirits; to another divers kinds of tongues; to another the interpretation of tongues," (1 Corinthians 12:8, 10).

The Holy Spirit gave Jeremiah photographs of his future from the Lord. "Then the word of the Lord came unto me, saying, Before I formed thee in the belly I knew thee; and before thou camest forth out of the womb I sanctified thee, and I ordained thee a prophet unto the nations," (Jeremiah 1:4-5).

The Holy Spirit is not a respecter of persons. Throughout the ages He has placed pictures of the future in the heart of those He loved. He will do it for you today.

God showed Abraham pictures of his future greatness. "And I will make of thee a great nation, and I will bless thee, and make thy name great; and thou shalt be a blessing: And I will bless them that bless thee, and curse him that curseth thee: and in thee shall all families of the earth be blessed," (Genesis 12:2-3).

You must *receive* a picture of your future.

You must *believe* that photograph.

You must *water* that Seed of Tomorrow.

You must receive it from The Holy Spirit.

You must *protect* that picture.

Nobody else can do it for you. Nobody else will believe it. You must embrace it, receive it, and *protect* that picture.

That incredible Photograph of Tomorrow is planted within you *by The Holy Spirit* who formed you even in your mother's womb.

The Holy Spirit gave Joseph a prophetic picture of his future in a dream. "For, behold, we were binding sheaves in the field, and, lo, my sheaf arose, and also stood upright; and, behold, your sheaves stood round about, and made obeisance to my sheaf," (Genesis 37:7).

Joseph saw himself in the position of authority. He saw others honoring him. His mind began to change. His conduct and behavior were altered to birth that picture.

What Happens In Your Mind Will Happen In Time.

That's why The Holy Spirit is so important in your life. Your behavior cannot change until He births in you a picture of what He is looking at when He sees you.

He *sees* something you do not see.

He is taking you where you have never been.

He is *planting the Seed* of what you are becoming.

He is the Spirit of prophecy...who is bringing the future into you: not merely you into your future.

Your Future Has To Move Into You Before You Can Move Into Your Future.

Your picture of tomorrow will impart a strength to endure your present tribulations and difficulties. Trouble becomes easier to handle when you know that it will not last forever. Jesus had this kind of picture—"Who for the joy that was set before Him endured the cross, despising the shame, and is set down at the right hand of the throne of God," (Hebrews 12:2).

Jesus had confidence in His resurrection and that enabled Him to endure His crucifixion.

Always remember, The Holy Spirit can reveal future events to you before they even happen.

Our Prayer Together...

"Father, You have a specific plan for my life. You already know what tomorrow holds. I *trust You*. So, I ask You to begin to show me *pictures* of Your future plans for me. Show me those Seeds of Tomorrow that I need to grow. Alter my conduct and my behavior so that it agrees with Your plan for my life. In Jesus' name. Amen."

➤ 21 ➤

THE HOLY SPIRIT PLACES AN UNCOMMON LOVE IN YOU FOR UNLOVABLE PEOPLE

Love Is The Most Powerful Force On Earth.

9 Facts You Should Know About Love

1. **The Holy Spirit Is The Source Of The Greatest Force On Earth—Love.** "Because the love of God is shed abroad in our hearts by the Holy Ghost which is given unto us," (Romans 5:5).

True love is not manipulating another.

True love is not decided by the conduct and behavior of another.

2. **Love Pursues.** "For the Son of man is come to seek and to save that which was lost," (Luke 19:10). (See also John 3:16 and Isaiah 1:18.)

3. **Love Protects.** "...for I the Lord thy God am a jealous God," (Exodus 20:5).

4. **Love Provides.** "...for I am the Lord that healeth thee," (Exodus 15:26).

5. **The Fruit Of The Holy Spirit Is Love.** "But the fruit of the Spirit is love," (Galatians 5:22). It is The Holy Spirit who places an unexplainable love within a mother's heart for her child; the husband's heart for his wife; the pastor's heart for his people.

6. **The Proof Of Love Is The Desire To**

Give. "For God so loved the world, that He gave His only begotten Son, that whosoever believeth in Him should not perish, but have everlasting life," (John 3:16). God gave. That proved His love.

   7.   The Holy Spirit Enabled Jesus To Love. He prayed, "Father, forgive them; for they know not what they do," (Luke 23:34).

   8.   The Holy Spirit Enabled Stephen To Love Those Who Stoned Him. "And he kneeled down, and cried with a loud voice, Lord, lay not this sin to their charge," (Acts 7:60). The Holy Spirit alone could plant this kind of love inside a human heart. It would have been normal to pray a prayer that called down fire from Heaven on those stoning you. This is a remarkable work of grace in the human heart. It is normal to retaliate. It is human to fight back. It is uncommon and divine to forgive. This is true love.

   Missionaries fight emotional battles, financial difficulties and cultural barriers because of the love of Christ within them for the heathen. I know many. They have forfeited the comforts and luxury of home to empty their lives into a small village. Why? The love of Christ placed there by The Holy Spirit for unlovable people.

   Many wives have birthed the salvation of their husbands because of the love of The Holy Spirit within them. Their husband came to Christ because of their conversation and conduct. *They never quit loving their husbands.*

   Thousands of rebellious teenagers have been drawn back home like a magnet to a loving parent... because of the love of The Holy Spirit. Certainly, parents have felt discouraged and demoralized. Anger is common among disappointed parents. But, The Holy Spirit can do the impossible—impart an uncommon love for a rebellious and stubborn teenager.

9.   God Sends His Love Toward You Even In The Worse Season Of Your Life. "But God commendeth His love toward us, in that, while we were yet sinners, Christ died for us" (Romans 5:8).

Here's a song I wrote to The Holy Spirit some time ago:

Love Words
Make all my words—Love Words;
Make all my words—Love Words;
That's what You made me for,
Holy Spirit, To pour your healing oil;
Make all my words—Your Love Words.

Always remember, The Holy Spirit places an uncommon love in you for unlovable people.

Our Prayer Together...
"Father, Your love is the most powerful force on earth. Show me *how* to love others as You would love them. I receive Your incredible love for my life with gratitude and thanksgiving. In Jesus' name. Amen."

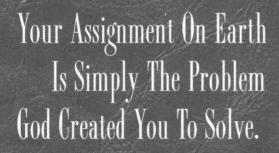

Your Assignment On Earth
Is Simply The Problem
God Created You To Solve.

-MIKE MURDOCK

⚈ 22 ⚈

THE HOLY SPIRIT DECIDES YOUR ASSIGNMENT, THE PROBLEM YOU WERE CREATED TO SOLVE

Your Assignment Has Already Been Decided.

The Holy Spirit decided your Assignment. "Before I formed thee in the belly I knew thee; and before thou camest forth out of the womb I sanctified thee, and I ordained thee a prophet unto the nations," (Jeremiah 1:5).

Jeremiah believed this. While he was yet in his mother's womb, God had decided that he would become a great deliverer. His responsibility? To accept it, not alter it.

Everything created contains an invisible instruction. Look inside a watermelon seed. You cannot see it with your natural eye. But, inside that watermelon seed is a command, an Assignment to produce more watermelons.

Everything created is a solution. Your eyes see. Your ears hear. Your hands reach. Your feet walk. Your mouth speaks. Mechanics solve car problems. Lawyers solve legal problems. Dentists solve teeth problems. Mothers solve emotional problems. Ministers solve spiritual problems.

You were created to solve some kind of problem while you are on the earth. The Holy Spirit created you (Job 33:4). He had a reason. That's why He gave you the specific gifts and talents that you have. "Now there are diversities of gifts, but the same Spirit. And there are differences of administrations, but the same Lord," (1 Corinthians 12:4-5).

You do not decide your gifts—you discover them. "But all these worketh that one and the selfsame Spirit, dividing to every man severally as He will," (1 Corinthians 12:11).

What you love is a clue to your Assignment. Think for a moment. What is your greatest passion? What excites you and energizes you every day? If you could speak on any one subject, what would that subject be? You see, whatever you love, you will have a Wisdom toward.

Love determines your Wisdom. A desire *to learn* will emerge toward whatever you have a love for. It may be animals, babies, or automobiles. Pay attention to the passion placed within your heart. It is a clue to your Assignment on earth.

What you hate is a clue to something you were created to correct or change. When Moses saw an Egyptian beating up an Israelite, an anger rose within him. Why? He was their Deliverer. You may hate alcohol, drugs, or child abuse. That is a clue to something you were created to change and correct.

What grieves you is a clue to something you were created to heal. Pay attention to your tears. Compassion is powerful. It is also a signpost to your Assignment on earth.

Your Assignment is geographical. The Holy Spirit knows exactly the town and city where you should live or minister. "Then the Spirit said unto Philip, go near, and join thyself to this chariot," (Acts 8:29; also see Acts 13:2).

Spiritual champions always depend on The Holy Spirit for specific instructions regarding their Assignment. "As they ministered to the Lord, and fasted, the Holy Ghost said, Separate Me Barnabas and Saul for the work whereunto I have called them. And when they had fasted and prayed, and laid their hands on them, they sent them away. So they, being sent forth by the Holy Ghost, departed unto Seleucia; and from thence they sailed to Cyprus," (Acts 13:2-4).

You must find the center of your expertise. Nobody else can find it for you. It may not be produced through your logic, questioning, nor even those special personality profile tests that you receive from particular counselors.

The Holy Spirit alone knows your Assignment. You will only discover it in His presence (Psalm 26:4-6).

Always remember, The Holy Spirit decides your Assignment, the problem you were created to solve.

Our Prayer Together...

"Holy Spirit, You created me for a reason. You know it and want to reveal it to me. Even now, I listen for Your voice. I will *go* anywhere You want me to go. I will *say* anything You want me to say. I will *stay* any place You want me to remain. *Your desires are my desires.* Remove from my life anything that is not of You. Take the wrong people out of my life. Bring the right people into my life. I accept and embrace totally and completely Your Assignment in my life today. In Jesus' name. Amen."

Those Who Unlock
  Your Compassion Are
Those To Whom You
  Have Been Assigned.

-MIKE MURDOCK

❧ 23 ❧
THE HOLY SPIRIT KNOWS TO WHOM YOU HAVE BEEN ASSIGNED

━━━━━❖━━━━━

Somebody Needs You.

The Holy Spirit decides your Assignment on earth. "Then the Spirit saith unto Philip, Go near, and join thyself to this chariot," (Acts 8:29).

You were created to solve a problem for somebody. Everything created is a solution to an existing problem. Your eyes see. Your ears hear. Your feet walk. Your mouth speaks. Mechanics solve car problems. Dentists solve teeth problem. Lawyers solve legal problems. Mothers solve emotional problems. Pastors solve spiritual problems. (See my book, *The Assignment: The Dream & The Destiny,* Volume 1, Chapter 22.)

You were created to solve a problem on earth.

The Holy Spirit knows where you belong.

He knows the person that He created you for.

Jeremiah discovered this. "Then said I, Ah, Lord God! behold, I cannot speak: for I am a child. But the Lord said unto me, Say not, I am a child: for thou shalt go to all that I shall send thee, and whatsoever I command thee thou shalt speak," (Jeremiah 1:6-7).

Philip, the Spirit-filled deacon, understood this.

The Holy Spirit led him away from Jerusalem, into the desert of Gaza. There, The Holy Spirit told him to "join thyself to this chariot," (Acts 8:29). It was here that the Ethiopian eunuch discovered Philip, and Philip discovered him. The Holy Spirit knows the *answers* you embrace—and the questions *others* are asking.

Oh, how desperately you and I need The Holy Spirit every day of our lives. Every minute can count. Every hour matters greatly. When you understand the importance of your Assignment, you will abandon yourself in totality to the voice of The Holy Spirit.

Jesus depended on The Holy Spirit completely. That's why He knew about the Samaritan woman waiting at the well. He "must needs go through Samaria" (John 4:4). There, He met the woman who had been married five times, but whose life was empty and lonely. Jesus promised her water. The Holy Spirit had directed His steps that day...*to the very person to whom He was assigned.*

The Holy Spirit will direct you away from unnecessary relationships. He removes distractions—people who would stop you from your Assignment.

The Holy Spirit will advise you about every appointment of the day. You see, every hour is a golden opportunity to be in the center of the will of God. When you are where God wants you, the provision is there for your life. Your sense of significance comes through total obedience and knowing you are where God has assigned you.

The Holy Spirit will reveal perfect timing. Timing is everything. Esther understood this when she approached the king. Because of her sensitivity about timing, God carefully led her into a strategy that would expose the evil heart of Haman. Haman wanted to assassinate all the Jews, but because of her careful leadership and timing, Esther saved her people.

Ruth understood this sense of timing. She was mentored by Naomi who emphasized the need for her to approach Boaz, her future husband, in a specific manner and way.

The Holy Spirit gives you the right words to say to those to whom you are assigned. You see, you can know your Assignment but not have the correct and appropriate approach to them. It makes all the difference in the world. "A soft answer turneth away wrath," (Proverbs 15:1).

The Holy Spirit will reveal to you what you should be doing for those to whom you are assigned. Sometimes, they only need a *listening* ear. Sometimes, they simply need your *words of caution* or encouragement. The Holy Spirit knows exactly *what they need.*

Always remember, The Holy Spirit knows to whom you have been assigned.

Our Prayer Together...

"Father, You have a Divine strategy for my life. I belong somewhere today. Somebody needs me.

I ask that Your words be placed in my mouth so that I can strengthen and encourage instead of harm and wound. You will direct every hour of today. I am counting on You completely. I trust You, Holy Spirit. In Jesus' name. Amen."

The Holy Spirit Is
The Only Person
You Are Required
To Obey.

-MIKE MURDOCK

∼ 24 ∼

THE HOLY SPIRIT IS NECESSARY FOR YOUR ENTRY INTO THE KINGDOM OF GOD

The Kingdom Of God Is A Mystery.

Logic cannot grasp it. Words cannot define it. Yet, millions have tasted the miraculous change from this world into the next world—*the new birth is a reality.* "But God hath chosen the foolish things of the world to confound the wise; and God hath chosen the weak things of the world to confound the things which are mighty; And base things of the world, and things which are despised, hath God chosen, yea, and things which are not, to bring to nought things that are," (1 Corinthians 1:27-28).

The kingdom of God is life in the Spirit. "For the kingdom of God is not meat and drink; but righteousness, and peace, and joy in the Holy Ghost," (Romans 14:17).

When your pursuit of His kingdom becomes your priority, everything else you need in life will emerge. "But seek ye first the kingdom of God, and His righteousness; and all these things shall be added unto you," (Matthew 6:33).

The kingdom of God is the opposite of the self-life. "Now the works of the flesh are manifest, which are these; Adultery, fornication, uncleanness, lasciviousness, Idolatry, witchcraft, hatred, variance, emulations, wrath, strife, seditions, heresies, Envyings, murders, drunkenness, revellings, and such like: of the which I tell you before, as I have also told you in time past, that they which do such things shall not inherit the kingdom of God," (Galatians 5:19-21).

You cannot enter life in the Spirit without respecting The Holy Spirit. He goes where He is desired, not merely where He is needed.

You cannot depart from an ungodly life without The Holy Spirit. "Wherein in time past ye walked according to the course of this world, according to the prince of the power of the air, the spirit that now worketh in the children of disobedience: Among whom also we all had our conversation in times past in the lusts of our flesh, fulfilling the desires of the flesh and of the mind; and were by nature the children of wrath, even as others," (Ephesians 2:2-3).

The mercy of God gives us access to The Holy Spirit who changes our very nature. "But God, who is rich in mercy, for His great love wherewith He loved us, Even when we were dead in sins, hath quickened us together with Christ, (by grace ye are saved;)" (Ephesians 2:4-5).

Millions are staggering around earth like drunkards emotionally bankrupt, spiritually sabotaged, helpless and lost. Only The Holy Spirit can move them from darkness into light.

The Holy Spirit is the only true Friend Who changes your very nature, gives you focus and turns you from a child of disobedience into a child of light.

Always remember, The Holy Spirit is necessary for

your entry into the kingdom of God.

Our Prayer Together...

"Heavenly Father, I thank You for caring enough for me to send The Holy Spirit to move me from darkness into light. I'm teachable. I'm willing to be corrected. I must change. I ask You to do a supernatural work of grace within me today. Holy Spirit, You are welcome in my life. Forgive me of any disobedience that has prevented me from entering into the Spirit life. I want to live as a child of Your kingdom. Your rulership is my desire. In Jesus' name. Amen."

God Creates Seasons;
Discoveries
   Schedule Them.

-*MIKE MURDOCK*

≈ 25 ≈

THE HOLY SPIRIT ONLY COMMITS HIS GUIDANCE TO THOSE WHO ARE TRUE SONS OF GOD

The Holy Spirit Always Rewards Obedience.

You cannot deceive Him. You cannot manipulate Him. You cannot intimidate Him. He rewards those who have accepted Christ as Lord and Savior...by Divine guidance and direction. "For as many as are led by the Spirit of God, they are the sons of God," (Romans 8:14).

Your commitment to Christ produces much more than eternal life in your future. Your life in Christ is honored and celebrated by The Holy Spirit who came to testify of Jesus and glorify Him.

Have you fully committed your life to Jesus? Have you determined with your whole heart to follow Him completely? He is the only Answer. There is no other answer to life than Jesus.

But, Jesus wants to rule every part of your life and guide you in the decisions you are making. He does this through the precious Holy Spirit who is our Adviser, Comforter, and Friend who never leaves us nor forsakes us.

Jesus said that the world did not really know

Him, and the ungodly would not recognize Him (read John 14, 15, 16). But, those who obeyed Him, He would guide and direct their decisions.

Ask Him to guide your decisions in every relationship. Avoid unholy alliances. "Can two walk together, except they be agreed?" (Amos 3:3).

Ask His guidance on every major financial purchase. The Holy Spirit knows the very home in which you should invest, the very car you should purchase. Yes, anything that concerns you will concern The Holy Spirit.

Ask His guidance about your spiritual overseer. Where do you belong? What church should you attend consistently? Where should your gifts be used the most? Who is the mentor The Holy Spirit has selected for you?

Ask His guidance about your career or place of business. Your work really matters to Him. Deuteronomy 28:12 says He will bless the "work of thine hand." So, seek His guidance. Never be ruled by logic. Logic can produce order, but faith produces miracles.

Accept and embrace the chain of authority The Holy Spirit has established in your life. Your parents are gifts from The Holy Spirit. Believe in God so strongly that you believe He can guide your life through their decisions. Submit yourself to those in your household that the Lord has established as those put in the place of responsibility over you. Expect The Holy Spirit to honor your humility and spirit of willingness.

Always remember, The Holy Spirit only commits His guidance to those who are true sons of God.

Our Prayer Together...

"Precious Father, thank You for every blessing You have given us, especially today, for the blessing of Divine guidance through The Holy Spirit. I trust You to guide me into a Place of Blessing. Guide me away from any place of temptation, unholy relationships, and where I could fall into error. Guide me concerning my spiritual pastor, my place of business, and even in my financial investments. I trust You. I lean on You. You will never disappoint me. My faith is wholly in You and because of that, I rest in peace today. In Jesus' name. Amen."

Aloneness Always
Concludes With
A Battle.

-MIKE MURDOCK

∾ 26 ∾

THE HOLY SPIRIT WILL OFTEN WARN YOU IN ADVANCE OF POSSIBLE DANGER

The Holy Spirit Is Your Personal Protector.

Your *safety* matters to Him. Your peace of mind matters to Him. He does not want you to waste your life or time with wrong places or dangerous people.

Nobody knows the map of your life as well as The Holy Spirit. That's why the apostle Paul counted on Him continuously. The Holy Spirit warned Paul through the prophets Ananias and Agabus (Acts 9 and Acts 21).

4 Facts The Holy Spirit Wants You To Remember About Your Enemy

1. Your Enemies Do Exist. You must recognize this. Satan has assigned people and empowered them with his evil and twisted power to break your focus and distract you from the perfect will of God.

2. Your Enemy Is Known Only By The Holy Spirit. Your enemy is deceptive, clever and cunning. He has prepared your downfall. You cannot afford to trust your own mind. "Trust in the Lord with all thine heart; and lean not unto thine own understanding. In all thy ways acknowledge Him, and He shall direct thy paths," (Proverbs 3:5-6).

3. When You Listen To The Holy Spirit, You Will Be Protected From The Pitfall Of Every Enemy. Continuously pray in the Spirit. Listen to His voice. When you are in the midst of a conversation with someone and sense satanic influence, stop and pray in the Spirit. (I have even left a restaurant table at times and gone to the washroom for the purpose of praying in The Holy Spirit privately. I sensed an evil power at work.)

4. Rest In The Knowledge That The Holy Spirit Will Continuously Warn You. Don't become unnerved, unsettled and angry. Simply rest and trust The Holy Spirit.

Always remember, The Holy Spirit will often warn you in advance of possible danger.

Our Prayer Together...

"Father, Your gift of protection is more important to me than anything in the world. I cannot survive alone. You know my enemy. So, I trust You completely today to warn me in every way when I am going the wrong way or when I enter into an alliance with wrong people. You are my Wall of Protection and I live protected by You. In Jesus' name. Amen."

❧ 27 ❧

THE HOLY SPIRIT IS GRIEVED BY WRONG CONVERSATION AND CONDUCT

The Holy Spirit Is Holy.

Words matter to Him. Conversation is important to Him. Your conduct and behavior is monitored continuously.

He will withdraw His manifest presence when He has been grieved and offended. That's why the apostle Paul wrote this remarkable warning: "Let no corrupt communication proceed out of your mouth, but that which is good to the use of edifying, that it may minister grace unto the hearers. *And grieve not The Holy Spirit of God*, whereby ye are sealed unto the day of redemption. Let all bitterness, and wrath, and anger, and clamour, and evil speaking, be put away from you, with all malice: And be ye kind one to another, tenderhearted, forgiving one another, even as God for Christ's sake hath forgiven you," (Ephesians 4:29-32).

Any untrue words that *wound* the *influence* of *someone not present* are *disloyal words*. Disloyalty is unholy. It is so important that you permit The Holy Spirit to correct you and prevent you from saying anything that is grievous to Him. His presence must be valued.

His presence brings joy. Peace. Calmness in spirit. You cannot afford a day without His presence.

I will never forget a conversation in Washington, DC. I came down from my hotel room full of joy and enthusiasm. I had been praying in the Spirit throughout the day. I could not remember happier hours or days in my life. When I sat down to eat, the name of someone came up. I was talking with two of my staff members. When this name came up, I made a statement: "I like the young man, but he is rather lazy." The conversation continued. And, after about one hour, I returned to my hotel room.

But, something was wrong. As I began to lift my hands and sing to The Holy Spirit, a cloud of heaviness settled into my heart. Something was out of order. So, not knowing what was wrong, I simply began to sing louder and become more aggressive in my worship.

The heaviness in my spirit remained. Suddenly, The Holy Spirit spoke to my heart: "Why did you tell them that this young man was lazy?"

I stopped. Then I replied almost defiantly to The Holy Spirit—"Well, because he *is* lazy!"

"You have offended Me," The Holy Spirit spoke into my heart.

I thought for a moment. Then I replied: "Well, he did not hear me anyway. He is over 1,000 miles away!"

"I heard you, and *you offended Me*."

I tried another approach. "Well, Lord, it is true that he is lazy and I would be willing to tell him to his face!"

Suddenly, The Holy Spirit stopped me with a

powerful understanding. He brought my mind to Philippians 4:8, where He gave us the criteria and guidelines for proper conversation:

▶ True

▶ Honest

▶ Just

▶ Pure

▶ Lovely

▶ Good report

▶ Virtuous

▶ Things praiseworthy

As He began to deal with my life, my heart began to break. I realized that I had spoken in a destructive way about someone who was precious to Him.

If something does not qualify for *meditation*, it does not quality for *conversation*. If it does not qualify for my *mind*, it does not qualify for my *mouth*.

Picture a mother showing you a photograph of her baby. Can you imagine her response to you if you began to sneer and make fun of the child, "What an ugly child! I despise that child!"

That mother would withdraw from you instantly.

You will see it happen in your own life every day. The moment you begin to discuss the flaws of *those not present*—The Holy Spirit will *withdraw*. "I will go and return to my place, till they acknowledge their offence," (Hosea 5:15).

When one of my staff members approached me, I asked what the appointment would be about. She wanted to talk about another staff member.

"Then, let's call her in to hear your accusation against her," I reached for the telephone.

"Oh no! I don't want her to hear what I'm saying! Let's just forget about it."

Imagine every church that would focus for twelve months only on encouraging conversation about others.

Imagine your family if every person would only speak well of each other.

You see, we have been taught to say good things about people because—"they may find out about it." But, that is not the only reason you must avoid wrong conversation. Others warn, "What goes around will come back around." That, too, is not the reason for avoiding destructive words about others.

The Holy Spirit is the reason you should avoid accusatory and unflattering conversation about others. He withdraws. His absence creates sorrow and heaviness of spirit.

Always remember, The Holy Spirit is grieved by wrong conversation and conduct.

Our Prayer Together...

"Heavenly Father, I have grieved You many times. I am so sorry. Please forgive me today. Remind me that others are important to You, also. I am not the only one in the family of God. In Jesus' name. Amen."

≈ 28 ≈

THE HOLY SPIRIT CRITIQUES EVERY MOMENT, MOTIVE AND MOVEMENT OF YOUR LIFE

The Holy Spirit Studies You.

Your motives are continuously monitored and evaluated. "For man looketh on the outward appearance, but the Lord looketh on the heart," (1 Samuel 16:7).

The apostle Paul mentions that our works would be evaluated by God's standard...not our own. Our works would burn up like wood and stubble...unless we have the right attitude. "Now if any man build upon this foundation gold, silver, precious stones, wood, hay, stubble; Every man's work shall be made manifest: for the day shall declare it, because it shall be revealed by fire; and the fire shall try every man's work of what sort it is. If any man's work abide which he hath built thereupon, he shall receive a reward. If any man's work shall be burned, he shall suffer loss: but he himself shall be saved; yet so as by fire," (1 Corinthians 3:12-15).

"Many will say to Me in that day, Lord, Lord, have we not prophesied in Thy name? and in Thy name have cast out devils? and in Thy name done many wonderful works? And then will I profess unto them, I never knew you: depart from Me, ye that work iniquity," (Matthew 7:22-23).

Eternity will reward those with pure hearts.

The Holy Spirit watches to schedule your deliverance from battle. "He hath delivered my soul in peace from the battle that was against me: for there were many with me. God shall hear, and afflict them, even he that abideth of old. Selah. Because they have no changes, therefore they fear not God," (Psalm 55:18-19). "For He hath delivered me out of all trouble: and mine eye hath seen His desire upon mine enemies," (Psalm 54:7). He did it for Jesus (Luke 4). *He did it for the Ethopian.*

The Holy Spirit watches for moments to lift your burden when you are too stressed. "Cast thy burden upon the Lord, and He shall sustain thee: He shall never suffer the righteous to be moved," (Psalm 55:22). He did it for the Ethiopian eunuch (Acts 8).

The Holy Spirit tests your appetite and pursuit of Him. "God looked down from heaven upon the children of men, to see if there were any that did understand, that did seek God," (Psalm 53:2). (Read Acts 8 regarding Philip and the eunuch.)

The Holy Spirit looks upon you to find a reason to bless you. "For the eyes of the Lord run to and fro throughout the whole earth, to shew Himself strong in the behalf of them whose heart is perfect toward Him. Herein thou hast done foolishly: therefore from henceforth thou shalt have wars," (2 Chronicles 16:9).

Always remember, The Holy Spirit critiques every moment, motive and movement of your life.

Our Prayer Together...
"Father, I am happy that You weigh my

thoughts and ways. Purge, purify and heal every broken area of my life. You are my Repairer. Convict my heart when I stray. Change me into what You want me to become. I cannot heal myself, but You will *perfect* that which concerns me. In Jesus' name. Amen."

An Uncontested Enemy
Will Flourish.

-MIKE MURDOCK

∾ 29 ∾

THE HOLY SPIRIT IS AN ENEMY TO ANY REBEL

>──●──<

The Holy Spirit Has A Dangerous Side.

The Holy Spirit can become an enemy to those who persist in rebellion. Rebellion infuriates The Holy Spirit. You see, The Holy Spirit is an example of agreement and cooperation. He stays in agreement with the Son and the Father. Unity is His trademark. Conflict angers Him. He is the Spirit of peace. He is the Spirit of love. He is the Spirit of Christ.

The Holy Spirit always responds to rebellion. "But they rebelled, and vexed His Holy Spirit: therefore He was turned to be their enemy, and He fought against them," (Isaiah 63:10).

The Holy Spirit woos. He draws us toward Him. He is merciful, gentle and kind. He is patient and long suffering. He labors over us as a mother would labor over a child in its tiny crib.

Oh, it is a fatal and deadly day when The Holy Spirit is finally vexed. First, He is quenched, then offended, grieved, and finally vexed. It seems that the season of vexation is the season before devastation. He turns on you. He decides to postpone His promotion for you.

That is a devastating day in any life.

His ministers are gifts that thousands refuse to

honor. They sneer, criticize and ignore. This is grievous to The Holy Spirit.

His miracles and continued protection are signs of mercy from Him. Yet, millions remain unthankful, ungrateful and continuously complain as if nothing good has ever occurred in their life.

Thousands refuse to permit conviction to do a deep work and change within them. Over a period of time, The Holy Spirit can become vexed. It is almost too late for a turnaround at this point.

Oh, I beg of you today! Listen to The Holy Spirit! Don't turn Him away! He is gentle as a dove, but He can become the Terror of Eternity! "How shall we escape, if we neglect so great salvation," (Hebrews 2:3).

Respond to His inner conviction and drawing. "...behold, now is the accepted time; behold, now is the day of salvation," (2 Corinthians 6:2).

8 Facts About Offending The Holy Spirit

1. Ignoring His Word Each Day Offends Him. "Study to shew thyself approved unto God, a workman that needeth not to be ashamed, rightly dividing the word of truth," (2 Timothy 2:15).

2. Careless And Useless Conversation Grieves Him. "But shun profane and vain babblings: for they will increase unto more ungodliness," (2 Timothy 2:16).

3. Continuous Resistance To The Holy Spirit Can Turn Him Into An Enemy. "Ye stiffnecked and uncircumcised in heart and ears, ye do always resist the Holy Ghost: as your fathers did, so do ye," (Acts 7:51).

4.   When You Ignore The Warnings Of The Holy Spirit, There Is No Other Source For Help. "For if we sin willfully after that we have received the knowledge of the truth, there remaineth no more sacrifice for sins, But a certain fearful looking for of judgment and fiery indignation, which shall devour the adversaries," (Hebrews 10:26-27).

5.   Disdain And Contempt In Attending The House Of God Offends The Holy Spirit. "Not forsaking the assembling of ourselves together, as the manner of some is; but exhorting one another: and so much the more, as you see the day approaching," (Hebrews 10:25).

6.   Developing   Companionship   And Relationships With Those Who Are Ungodly And Rebellious Toward Truth Offends The Holy Spirit. "And have no fellowship with the unfruitful works of darkness, but rather reprove them," (Ephesians 5:11).

7.   Any Word That Does Not Edify And Strengthen Others Can Become Grievous To The Holy Spirit. "Let no corrupt communication proceed out of your mouth, but that which is good to the use of edifying, that it may minister grace unto the hearers. And grieve not The Holy Spirit of God, whereby ye are sealed unto the day of redemption. Let all bitterness, and wrath, and anger, and clamour, and evil speaking, be put away from you, with all malice: And be ye kind one to another, tenderhearted, forgiving one another, even as God for *Christ's* sake hath forgiven you," (Ephesians 4:29-32).

8.   Permitting Others To Deceive You With Error And Falsehood Infuriates The Holy Spirit.

"Let no man deceive you with vain words: for because of these things cometh the wrath of God upon the children of disobedience. Be not ye therefore partakers with them," (Ephesians 5:6-7).

The anger of The Holy Spirit is seen within days of the first outpouring on the Day of Pentecost. The Holy Spirit killed a man and his wife...right in the church services. Read Acts 5. It's shocking, important and revealing. The Holy Spirit despises lying. He hates deception. He can react in a moment in a fierce way. Peter asked, "Why hath satan filled thine heart to lie to the Holy Ghost, and to keep back part of the price of the land?...thou hast not lied unto men, but unto God," (Acts 5:3-4).

Ananias fell down. Dead.

Then, great fear "came on all of them that heard these things." After his burial, his wife came in. She lied also. "Then fell she down straightway at his feet, and yielded up the ghost: and the young men came in, and found her dead, and, carrying her forth, buried her by her husband," (Acts 5:10).

Why does The Holy Spirit deal so strongly with rebellion? To bring us into the *fear of God.* "And great fear came upon all the church, and upon as many as heard these things," (Acts 5:11).

On the wall of my Secret Place is one of the most important truths in the Bible. "Let us hear the conclusion of the whole matter: Fear God, and keep His commandments: for this is the whole duty of man. For God shall bring every work into judgment, with every secret thing, whether it be good, or whether it be evil," (Ecclesiastes 12:13-14).

Oh, hear me today, precious friend! You may be

disappointed in yourself. Ministers may have failed to live the high standard you anticipated or expected. Your parents may have disappointed you. But, when you turn your anger and contempt toward The Holy Spirit, you will schedule the most desolate and destructive seasons of your lifetime.

You cannot afford for The Holy Spirit to become your enemy.

You may *sneer* at the standards of holiness established by some.

You may *laugh* with glee at the various teachings of religion.

You may *find flaws* in the most perfect church you have ever attended.

But, *you will stand before God and give an account for every response* you have made to the inner voice of The Holy Spirit. "So then every one of us shall give account of himself to God," (Romans 14:12).

Your conscience could become one of the best friends you have ever had. Listen to The Holy Spirit.

He talks to you through your *conscience*.

He will talk to you through your *pastor*.

He will communicate through your *parents*.

He will mentor you through His *principles*.

Whatever you do, honor and treasure the voice of the precious Holy Spirit in your life today!

Many years ago, Kathryn Kuhlman wept and sobbed as she looked across the congregation and begged and pleaded, "Please don't grieve The Holy Spirit! Please do not grieve The Holy Spirit!" The crowd was stunned. Many did not understand what she was talking about. But, those who know His presence admit there is nothing any more wonderful than the pleasure of His presence.

Obey Him.

Obey Him *swiftly*.

Obey Him *completely*.

Have you made any vows to your church or a man of God? Oh, swiftly *run*...swiftly run...swiftly run...*to complete those vows today.*

Always remember, The Holy Spirit is an enemy to any rebel.

Our Prayer Together...

"Holy Spirit, forgive me for anything that I have done to offend You and for ignoring Your inner voice. Cleanse, purge and remove anything in me that is unlike You. Reveal Yourself again to me. In Jesus' name. Amen."

≋ 30 ≋

THE HOLY SPIRIT MAY WITHDRAW HIS MANIFEST PRESENCE WHEN HE HAS BEEN OFFENDED

⇒≋◉≋⇐

Never Take His Presence Lightly.

"I will go and return to My place, till they acknowledge their offence, and seek My face: in their affliction they will seek Me early," (Hosea 5:15). "Let no corrupt communication proceed out of your mouth, but that which is good to the use of edifying, that it may minister grace unto the hearers, And grieve not The Holy Spirit of God, whereby ye are sealed unto the day of redemption, Let all bitterness, and wrath, and anger, and clamour, and evil speaking, be put away from you, with all malice: And be ye kind one to another, tenderhearted, forgiving one another, even as God for Christ's sake hath forgiven you," (Ephesians 4:29-32).

The love of God has been so misunderstood. His mercy has been taken for granted by millions.

"Oh, well! God knows my heart," laughed one lady when her pastor asked her why she had not been to church in several months. She had been taking vacations, spending her time out on the lake on Sundays. Yet, she had become so accustomed to ignoring the inner voice of The Holy Spirit, her conscience had become seared and numb.

It is a dangerous moment to think that access to God is permanent and easy.

His presence keeps you soft toward Him.

His presence keeps you hungry and thirsty. When you do not pursue His presence, the danger of becoming calloused and hardened is very real. A minister once told me, "I never dreamed I could get this far from God." As I looked at him, I was shocked. Here sat a man who had preached with fire in his soul, love pouring through his heart, many years before.

But, he had offended The Holy Spirit. Over and over again. Now, The Holy Spirit had withdrawn from him. He had even lost his hunger and his thirst for the presence of God.

When you feel troubled in your spirit, thank God for such a troubling. Millions have ignored Him so long that the fire of desire has died out. Only ashes remain.

Rejection of The Holy Spirit can be fatal. Jesus said it clearly, "Remember Lot's wife," (Luke 17:32). The angels had appeared personally to escort Lot and his family from danger to safety. But, she took it lightly. Their instructions became unimportant. She rebelled and did what she desired. She became a pillar of salt.

Jesus wept over Jerusalem. "O Jerusalem, Jerusalem, thou that killest the prophets, and stonest them which are sent unto thee, how often would I have gathered thy children together, even as a hen gathereth her chickens under her wings, and ye would not!" (Matthew 23:37).

Rejection of Him always produces desolation. "Behold, your house is left unto you desolate," (Matthew 23:38).

Conversation can grieve The Holy Spirit. "Let no corrupt communication proceed out of your mouth, but that which is good to the use of edifying, that it may minister grace unto the hearers. And grieve not The Holy Spirit of God, whereby ye are sealed unto the day of redemption," (Ephesians 4:29-30).

The presence of The Holy Spirit yesterday does not guarantee the presence of God tomorrow. Look at what happened to Saul. He had known the Anointing. God had selected him. God had touched his life. The prophet of God anointed him. Yet, "the Spirit of the Lord departed from Saul, and an evil spirit from the Lord troubled him," (1 Samuel 16:14).

He died the death of a fool.

The psalmist knew the terrifying seasons when The Holy Spirit seemed withdrawn from him. David had been with Saul. He watched evil spirits depart as he played his harp. He saw the touch of God on Saul come...*and leave.* He cried out after his own terrible sin with Bathsheba, "Cast me not away from Thy presence; and take not Thy Holy Spirit from me," (Psalm 51:11). Now, theologians laugh at David's confession and pursuit. Thousands of ministers say David was wrong, that The Holy Spirit could not withdraw from him. But, David had observed King Saul's deterioration. Don't kid yourself.

If you have spent much time on the earth, as a minister of the gospel, you will see many from whom The Holy Spirit has withdrawn. No, He doesn't do it easily or quickly. He is long-suffering. He is patient.

But, *repeated rejection of His drawing has devastating results.*

Most have never read these terrifying words in Hosea 5:15: "I will go and return to My place, til they acknowledge their offense, and seek My face: In their affliction, they will seek Me early."

I raise my voice with Hosea today: "Come, and let us return unto the Lord: for He hath torn, and He will heal us; He hath smitten, and He will bind us up. After two days will He revive us: in the third day He will raise us up, and we shall live in His sight. Then shall we know, if we follow on to know the Lord," (Hosea 6:1-3).

The Song of Solomon contains one of the saddest photographs of love rejected and lost. "I opened to my beloved; but my beloved had withdrawn himself, and was gone: my soul failed when he spake, I sought him, but I could not find him; I called him, but he gave me no answer," (Song of Solomon 5:6).

Now, *satan often lies to someone about the withdrawing of The Holy Spirit.* He makes them feel that it is useless to pray, futile to reach, and hopeless to believe for a change. Satan often tells people that they have sinned "the unpardonable sin" when the opposite is true.

How do you know that you have not truly sinned the unpardonable sin? *If you still have a desire for Him, The Holy Spirit is at work.* The Father is the One who draws you. If you still have within your heart a sincere desire to know God and an appetite to pursue Him, you have not yet sinned the unpardonable sin. You see, only God can draw you. If He is drawing you, it is not too late.

You still have a chance for a miraculous *experience* with Him.

Always remember, The Holy Spirit may withdraw His manifest presence when He has been offended.

Our Prayer Together...

"Heavenly Father, I am teachable today. I am reachable today. Cleanse me, purify me, and draw me toward You. I do not want to take lightly Your presence and the access I have to You. In my failures, You have sustained me and kept alive within me a desire for righteousness. This craving and desire for perfection has come from You, not myself. I ask You to draw me to You today more than You ever have. Turn my heart toward You. Birth within me a hatred for unrighteousness and a love for holy living. You are my God, and I am Your child. In Jesus' name. Amen."

Your Testing Qualifies
You For A Promotion.
Your Promotion Qualifies
You For Rewards.
Your Rewards Increase The
Flow Of Your Joy.

-MIKE MURDOCK

⁓ 31 ⁓
THE HOLY SPIRIT SHALL GIVE YOU STRENGTH WHEN A BATTLE HAS LEFT YOU WEAK

The Holy Spirit Imparts Power.
When your battle has left you drained and empty and you can't rise, The Holy Spirit enters.

"He giveth power to the faint; and to them that have no might He increaseth strength. Even the youths shall faint and be weary, and the young men shall utterly fall: But they that wait upon the Lord shall renew their strength; they shall mount up with wings as eagles; they shall run, and not be weary; and they shall walk, and not faint," (Isaiah 40:29-31).

People drain you. Battles drain you. You must go back to The Holy Spirit for rejuvenation. Stop looking for people to encourage you. Encourage yourself in the Lord.

You have an Encourager inside you. Stop waiting for others to speak good things about you. "Delight thyself also in the Lord; and He shall give thee the desires of thine heart," (Psalm 37:4).

Jesus promised that power would come to us through The Holy Spirit. "But ye shall receive power, after that the Holy Ghost is come upon you: and ye shall be witnesses unto me both in Jerusalem, and in all Judaea, and in Samaria, and unto the uttermost part of the earth," (Acts 1:8).

You will see your deliverance from the battle. "Notwithstanding the Lord stood with me, and strengthened me; that by me the preaching might be fully known, and that all the Gentiles might hear: and I was delivered out of the mouth of the lion. And the Lord shall deliver me from every evil work, and will preserve me unto His heavenly kingdom: to whom be glory for ever and ever," (2 Timothy 4:17-18).

The Holy Spirit becomes an enemy to your enemies. "But if thou shalt indeed obey His voice, and do all that I speak; then I will be an enemy unto thine enemies, and an adversary unto thine adversaries," (Exodus 23:22).

The Holy Spirit will raise up a standard like a flood. "When the enemy shall come in like a flood, the Spirit of the Lord shall lift up a standard against him," (Isaiah 59:19).

You will experience a supernatural rest from your warfare. "...for so He giveth His beloved sleep," (Psalm 127:2).

Always remember, The Holy Spirit shall give you strength when a battle has left you weak.

Our Prayer Together...

"Father, You have observed the warfare around me. You are aware of my enemies. Jesus promised The Holy Spirit would impart power to my life. I receive that promise today. In Jesus' name. Amen."

Clip and Mail

DECISION

Will You Accept Jesus As Your Personal Savior Today?

The Bible says, "That if thou shalt confess with thy mouth the Lord Jesus, and shalt believe in thine heart that God hath raised Him from the dead, thou shalt be saved," (Romans 10:9).

Pray this prayer from your heart today!

"Dear Jesus, I believe that You died for me and rose again on the third day. I confess I am a sinner...I need Your love and forgiveness...Come into my heart. Forgive my sins. I receive Your eternal life. Confirm Your love by giving me peace, joy and supernatural love for others. Amen."

DR. MIKE MURDOCK

is in tremendous demand as one of the most dynamic speakers in America today.

More than 16,000 audiences in 40 countries have attended his Schools of Wisdom and conferences. Hundreds of invitations come to him from churches, colleges and business corporations. He is a noted author of over 200 books, including the best sellers, *The Leadership Secrets of Jesus* and *Secrets of the Richest Man Who Ever Lived.* Thousands view his weekly television program, *Wisdom Keys with Mike Murdock.* Many attend his Schools of Wisdom that he hosts in many cities of America.

☐ Yes, Mike! I made a decision to accept Christ as my personal Savior today. Please send me my free gift of your book, *31 Keys to a New Beginning* to help me with my new life in Christ.

NAME BIRTHDAY

ADDRESS

CITY STATE ZIP

PHONE E-MAIL

Mail to: **The Wisdom Center** · 4051 Denton Hwy. · Ft. Worth, TX 76117 USA · 1-817-759-BOOK · 1-817-759-0300

You Will Love Our Website...! www.WisdomOnline.com

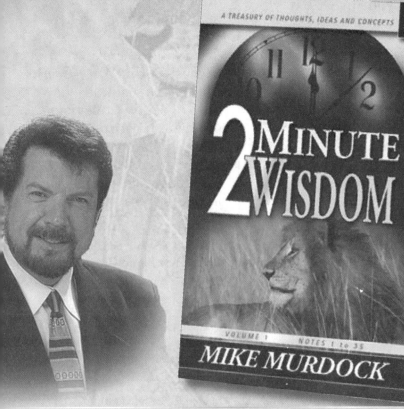

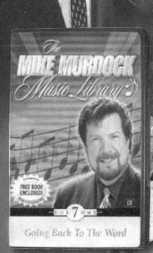
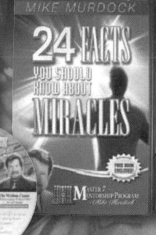

Don't Miss An Issue Of
The Wisdom Digest

Dr. Murdock's Quarterly Magazine Full of Wisdom, Inspiration and Upcoming Events At The Wisdom Center

Ask For Your Subscription Today!

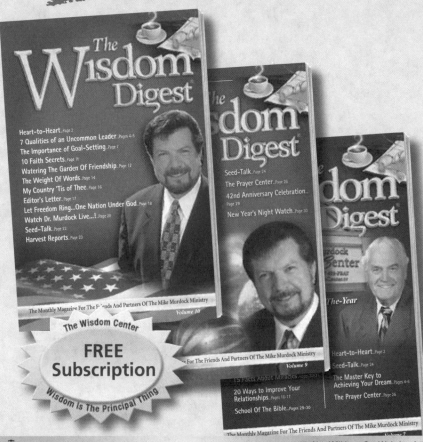

The Wisdom Center

FREE Subscription

Wisdom Is The Principal Thing

Which Two Friends Deserve A Free Subscription To The Wisdom Digest?

A miracle is in your hands

EVERY ISSUE OF THE WISDOM DIGEST CONTAINS A SPECIAL PRAYER REQUEST SECTION...ON THE ENCLOSED POSTAGE-PAID ENVELOPE...for you to return to me and The Prayer Team here at The Wisdom Center. Twice a day your Prayer Requests are presented to the Lord. Invest the time to mail your Prayer Agreement Page to me or email me at praynow@thewisdomcenter.tv. Your miracle is in your hand.

When You Respect Your Intercessors, Your Life Will Experience The Greatest Parade Of Miracles You Ever Dreamed Possible.

the wisdom digest to a friend

Yes Mike, I would like my friend(s) to receive *The Wisdom Digest*.

☐

NAME

ADDRESS

CITY   STATE   ZIP

PHONE   E-MAIL

☐

NAME

ADDRESS

CITY   STATE   ZIP

PHONE   E-MAIL

Enclosed is My Special Seed of $_____ for your Ministry. Please continue to send my own Gift Subscription of The Wisdom Digest to the address below.

Method of Payment (your transaction may be electronically deposited)

☐ MONEY ORDER ☐ CHECK ☐ VISA
☐ MASTER CARD ☐ AMEX   ☐ DISCOVER

CARD # _____-_____-_____-_____
EXP. DATE ___/___   TOTAL ENCLOSED $_____
SIGNATURE _____

(SORRY NO C.O.D.'S)

Your Seed Faith Offerings are used to support The Wisdom Center, and all its programs. Applicable law requires that we have the discretion to allocate donations in order to carry out our charitable purpose. In the event The Wisdom Center receives more funds for the project than needed, the excess will be used for another worthy outreach.

NAME

ADDRESS

CITY   STATE   ZIP

PHONE   E-MAIL

The Wisdom Center, 4051 Denton Highway, Ft. Worth, TX 76117
Ph: (817) 759-BOOK • (817) 759-0300 • Fx: (817) 759-0310

THE WISDOM CENTER
4051 Denton Highway • Fort Worth TX 76117

1-817-759-BOOK
1-817-759-0300

You Will Love Our Website...I
www.WisdomOnline.com

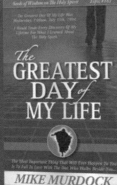

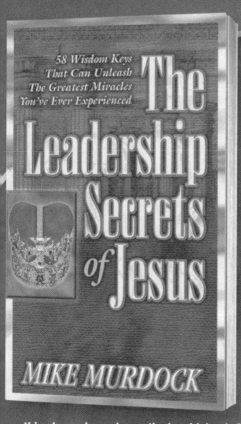

Millionaire-Talk

DR. MIKE MURDOCK

31 Things You Will Need To Become A Millionaire (CD/MT-20)

Topics Include:

- *You Will Need Financial Heroes*
- *Your Willingness To Negotiate Everything*
- *You Must Have The Ability To Transfer Your Enthusiasm, Your Vision To Others*
- *Know Your Competition*
- *Be Willing To Train Your Team Personally As To Your Expectations*
- *Hire Professionals To Do A Professional's Job*

I have asked the Lord for 3,000 special partners who will sow an extra Seed of $58 towards the Ministry Outreaches. Your Seed is so appreciated! Remember to request this Gift CD, *31 Things You Will Need To Become A Millionaire,* when you write this week!

THE WISDOM CENTER
4051 Denton Highway • Fort Worth, TX 76117
1-817-759-BOOK
1-817-759-0300
— *You Will Love Our Website...!* —
www.WisdomOnline.com
A

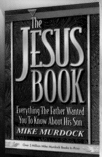

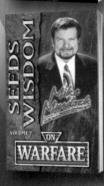

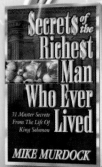

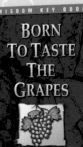

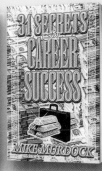
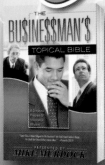

101 Wisdom Keys That Have Most Changed My Life.

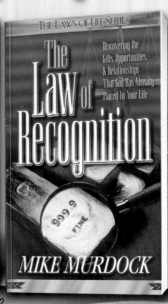

The Laws Of Life Series

The Law of Recognition

Discovering the Gifts, Opportunities, & Relationships That God Has Already Placed In Your Life

MIKE MURDOCK

SERIES 2

The **SCHOOL** *of* **WISDOM**

101 WISDOM KEYS THAT HAVE MOST CHANGED MY LIFE

MIKE MURDOCK

TS-42

101 WISDOM KEYS THAT HAVE MOST CHANGED MY LIFE

DR. MIKE MURDOCK

School of Wisdom #2 Pak!

▶ What Attracts Others Toward You

▶ The Secret Of Multiplying Your Financial Blessings

▶ What Stops The Flow Of Your Faith

▶ Why Some Fail And Others Succeed

▶ How To Discern Your Life Assignment

▶ How To Create Currents Of Favor With Others

▶ How To Defeat Loneliness

▶ 47 Keys In Recognizing The Mate God Has Approved For You

▶ 14 Facts You Should Know About Your Gifts And Talents

▶ 17 Important Facts You Should Remember About Your Weakness

▶ And Much, Much More...

The Wisdom Center
School of Wisdom #2 Pak!
Only **$30** $40 Value
PAK002
Wisdom Is The Principal Thing

Add 10% For S/H

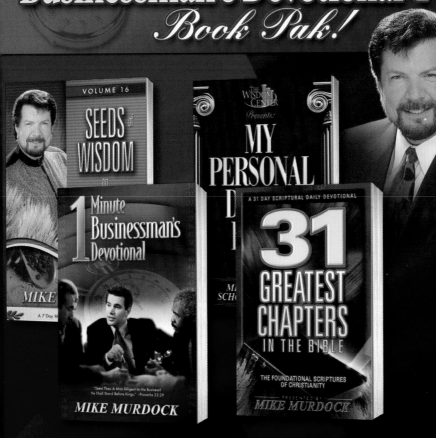

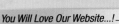

THE TURNAROUND Collection

❶ The Wisdom Commentary Vol. 1 (Book/B-136/256pg/52 Topics/$20)

❷ Battle Techniques For War-Weary Saints (Book/B-07/32pg/$5)

❸ Seeds of Wisdom on Overcoming (Book/B-17/32pg/$3)

❹ The Memory Bible on Healing (Book/B-196/32pg/$3)

❺ How To Turn Your Mistakes Into Miracles (Book/B-56/32pg/$5)

❻ 7 Keys To Turning Your Life Around (DVD/MMPL-03D/$10)

❼ The Sun Will Shine Again (Music CD/MMML-01/$10)

The Wisdom Center
The Turnaround Collection
Only $**40** $56 Value
PAK-15
Wisdom Is The Principal Thing

Add 10% For S/H

Each Wisdom Book may be purchased separately if so desired.

 **THE WISDOM CENTER** 4051 Denton Highway • Fort Worth, TX 76117

1-817-759-BOOK
1-817-759-0300

You Will Love Our Website...!
www.WisdomOnline.com

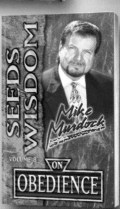

Financial $ecrets.

The Wisdom Center
Buy One... Receive The Second One FREE!
Wisdom Is The Principal Thing

VI-17

VI-16

Your Financial World Will Change Forever.

Video 2-Pak!

▶ 8 Scriptural Reasons You Should Pursue Financial Prosperity

▶ The Secret Prayer Key You Need When Making A Financial Request To God

▶ The Weapon Of Expectation And The 5 Miracles It Unlocks

▶ How To Discern Those Who Qualify To Receive Your Financial Assistance

▶ How To Predict The Miracle Moment God Will Schedule Your Financial Break through

▶ Habits Of Uncommon Achievers

▶ The Greatest Success Law I Ever Discovered

▶ How To Discern Your Place Of Assignment, The Only Place Financial Provision Is Guaranteed

▶ 3 Secret Keys In Solving Problems For Others

The Wisdom Center
Video 2-Pak!
Only $**30** $60 Value
VIPAK-01
Wisdom Is The Principal Thing

Add 10% For S/H

Each Wisdom Product may be purchased separately if so desired.

THE WISDOM CENTER
4051 Denton Highway • Fort Worth, TX 76117
1-817-759-BOOK
1-817-759-0300

You Will Love Our Website...!
www.WisdomOnline.com

K

THE WISDOM BIBLE

Partnership Edition

Over 120 Wisdom Study Guides Included Such As:

- ► 10 Qualities Of Uncommon Achievers
- ► 18 Facts You Should Know About The Anointing
- ► 21 Facts To Help You Identify Those Assigned To You
- ► 31 Facts You Should Know About Your Assignment
- ► 8 Keys That Unlock Victory In Every Attack
- ► 22 Defense Techniques To Remember During Seasons Of Personal Attack
- ► 20 Wisdom Keys And Techniques To Remember During An Uncommon Battle
- ► 11 Benefits You Can Expect From God
- ► 31 Facts You Should Know About Favor
- ► The Covenant Of 58 Blessings
- ► 7 Keys To Receiving Your Miracle
- ► 16 Facts You Should Remember About Contentious People
- ► 5 Facts Solomon Taught About Contracts
- ► 7 Facts You Should Know About Conflict
- ► 6 Steps That Can Unlock Your Self-Confidence
- ► And Much More!

   Your Partnership makes such a difference in The Wisdom Center Outreach Ministries. I wanted to place a Gift in your hand that could last a lifetime for you and your family...**The Wisdom Study Bible.**

   40 Years of Personal Notes...this Partnership Edition Bible contains 160 pages of my Personal Study Notes...that could forever change your Bible Study of The Word of God. This **Partnership Edition...**is my personal **Gift of Appreciation** when you sow your Sponsorship Seed of $1,000 to help us complete The Prayer Center and TV Studio Complex. An Uncommon Seed Always Creates An Uncommon Harvest!

Mike

Thank you from my heart for your Seed of Obedience (Luke 6:38).

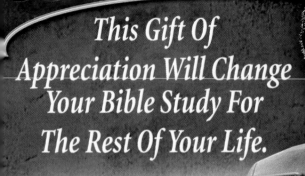

This Gift Of Appreciation Will Change Your Bible Study For The Rest Of Your Life.

The Wisdom Bible

MY GIFT OF APPRECIATION
Celebrating Your Sponsorship Seed of $1,000 For The Prayer Center & TV Studio Complex
B-235
Wisdom Is The Principal Thing

Spirit Music.

The Mike Murdock Music Library

LOVE SONGS TO THE HOLY SPIRIT

Written In The Secret Place

TS-59

LOVE SONGS TO THE HOLY SPIRIT
DR. MIKE MURDOCK

THE HOLY SPIRIT HANDBOOK

What You Need To Know About Your Daily Companion, The Holy Spirit

MR...

The Wisdom Center
Free Book
ENCLOSED!
B-100 ($10 Value)
Wisdom Is The Principal Thing

Songs...

1. A Holy Place
2. Anything You Want
3. Everything Comes From You
4. Fill This Place With Your Presence
5. First Thing Every Morning
6. Holy Spirit, I Want To Hear You
7. Holy Spirit, Move Again
8. Holy Spirit, You Are Enough
9. I Don't Know What I Would Do Without You
10. I Let Go (Of Anything That Stops Me)
11. I'll Just Fall On You
12. I Love You, Holy Spirit
13. I'm Building My Life Around You
14. I'm Giving Myself To You
15. I'm In Love! I'm In Love!
16. I Need Water (Holy Spirit, You're My Well)
17. In The Secret Place

18. In Your Presence, I'm Always Changed
19. In Your Presence (Miracles Are Born)
20. I've Got To Live In Your Presence
21. I Want To Hear Your Voice
22. I Will Do Things Your Way
23. Just One Day At A Time
24. Meet Me In The Secret Place
25. More Than Ever Before
26. Nobody Else Does What You Do
27. No No Walls!
28. Nothing Else Matters Anymore (Since I've Been In The Presence Of You Lord)
29. Nowhere Else
30. Once Again You've Answered
31. Only A Fool Would Try (To Live Without You)
32. Take Me Now
33. Teach Me How To Please You

34. There's No Place I'd Rather B
35. Thy Word Is All That Matters
36. When I Get In Your Presence
37. You're The Best Thing (That's Ever Happened To Me)
38. You Are Wonderful
39. You've Done It Once
40. You Keep Changing Me
41. You Satisfy

The Wisdom Center
6 Tapes/Only $30*
PAK007
Wisdom Is The Principal Thing

Add 10% For S/H

JOIN THE Wisdom Key 3000 TODAY!

Will You Become My Ministry Partner In The Work Of God?

Dear Friend,

God has connected us!

I have asked The Holy Spirit for 3000 Special Partners who will plant a monthly Seed of $58.00 to help me bring the gospel around the world. (58 represents 58 kinds of blessings in the Bible.)

Will you become my monthly Faith Partner in The Wisdom Key 3000? Your monthly Seed of $58.00 is so powerful in helping heal broken lives. When you sow into the work of God, 4 Miracle Harvests are guaranteed in Scripture, Isaiah 58...

▶ Uncommon <u>Health</u> (Isaiah 58)
▶ Uncommon <u>Wisdom</u> For <u>Decision-Making</u> (Isaiah 58)
▶ Uncommon <u>Financial Favor</u> (Isaiah 58)
▶ Uncommon <u>Family Restoration</u> (Isaiah 58)

Your Faith Partner,

Mike Murdock

P.S. Please clip the coupon attached and return it to me today, so I can rush the Wisdom Key Partnership Pak to you...or call me at 1-817-759-0300.

PP-03

☐ **Yes Mike, I want to join The Wisdom Key 3000. Please rush The Wisdom Key Partnership Pak to me today!**

☐ **Enclosed is my first monthly Seed-Faith Promise of:**
    ☐ **$58** ☐ **Other $_____.**

☐ CHECK ☐ MONEY ORDER ☐ AMEX ☐ DISCOVER ☐ MASTERCARD ☐ VISA

Credit Card # _____ Exp. ____/____

Signature _____

Name _____ Birth Date ____/____

Address _____

City _____ State _____ Zip _____

Phone _____ E-Mail _____

Your Seed-Faith offerings are used to support The Wisdom Center and all its programs. Your transaction may be electronically deposited. The Wisdom Center reserves the right to redirect funds as needed in order to carry out our charitable purpose.

P | **THE WISDOM CENTER** 4051 Denton Highway • Fort Worth, TX 76117 | **1-817-759-BOOK** **1-817-759-0300** | — You Will Love Our Website...! — **www.WisdomOnline.com**